WORKSHOP
IDEA BOOK

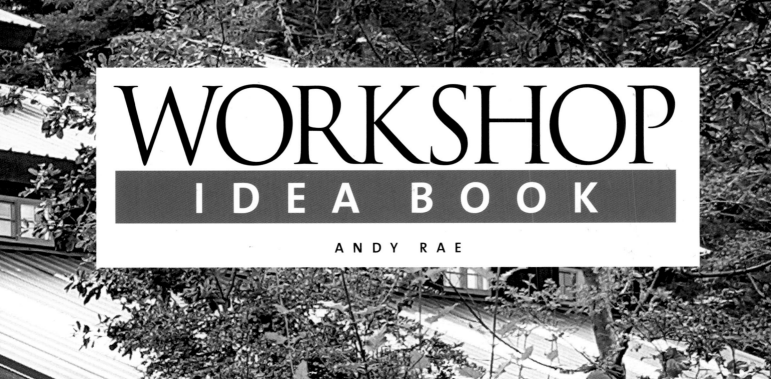

WORKSHOP
IDEA BOOK

ANDY RAE

The Taunton Press

The Taunton Press
Inspiration for hands-on living®

The Taunton Press, Inc., 63 South Main Street, PO Box 5506, Newtown, CT 06470-5506
e-mail: tp@taunton.com

EDITOR: Jennifer Renjilian Morris
INTERIOR DESIGN: Lori Wendin
LAYOUT: Laura Lind Design
ILLUSTRATOR: Christine Erikson
FRONT COVER PHOTOGRAPHERS: (top row, left to right): Andy Rae; Matt Berger, courtesy *Fine Woodworking,*
© The Taunton Press, Inc.; Mike Pekovich, courtesy *Fine Woodworking,* © The Taunton Press, Inc.;
(middle row, left to right): Andy Rae; © Jim Moon; Asa Christiana, courtesy *Fine Woodworking,* © The
Taunton Press, Inc.; (bottom row, left to right): Andy Rae.
BACK COVER PHOTOGRAPHER: Andy Rae

Library of Congress Cataloging-in-Publication Data

Rae, Andy.
  Workshop idea book / Andy Rae.
     p. cm.
  ISBN 1-56158-695-1
  1. Workshops--Design and construction. 2. Woodwork. I. Title: Workshop idea book. II. Title.
  TT152.R34 2005
  684'.08--dc22

                          2005000548

Printed in the Singapore
10 9 8 7 6 5 4 3 2 1

The following manufacturers/names appearing in *Workshop Idea Book* are trademarks: ADJUSTABENCH®,
Bessey K Body®, Kevlar®

Working wood is inherently dangerous. Using hand or power tools improperly or ignoring safety practices can lead to permanent
injury or even death. Don't try to perform operations you learn about here (or elsewhere) unless you're certain they are safe for
you. If something about an operation doesn't feel right, don't do it. Look for another way. We want you to enjoy the craft, so
please keep ssafety foremost in your mind whenever you're in the shop.

Acknowledgments

How do you write a book about cool woodworking stuff for the shop? Call on woodworkers, that's how. This book came to fruition because of the woodworkers around the country who showed me their best shop ideas. My sincerest gratitude goes to all those shop owners who bravely opened their own personal workspaces to let me in and then let me hound them with questions, sketch unusual ideas, and photograph their clever designs. Thanks also to those woodworkers who sent photos and notes to me from shops too distant to visit. All combined, the ideas in this book represent hundreds of years of collective woodworking wisdom and prove that a lone woodworker cannot dream up the best ideas on his own. My job was simply to motivate the woodworking community and then put it all together in a sensible manner to fill the pages. Thanks, all my old and new woodworker friends, for sharing.

I also want to express my gratitude to the publishers, editors, and photography and art staff at The Taunton Press. This book was a whirlwind of tight deadlines, from time-crunched photo shoots and all-night writing to unforeseen space constraints and logistical problem solving that no single author could have sanely faced alone. The folks at Taunton never quit on me. Special thanks to Helen Albert, executive editor, and Julie Hamilton, project editor, who both kept the hotline open 24/7. My appreciation also goes to my two editors, Jennifer Renjilian Morris and Robyn Doyon-Aitken, plus the talented editorial assistant, Jenny Peters, who all kept a watchful eye on my Ps and Qs and made sure all the paperwork got done in as timely and sensible a manner as possible.

As always, my family is my biggest supporter. Without their daily connection, no work could be done. Thanks, Lee, Zy, and Shade, for being here.

This book is dedicated to woodworker and savvy shop rat, Steve Blenk, a tall man with even taller goodwill. He will never leave those that knew him.

Contents

Introduction ▪ 2

Chapter 1
What Makes a Good Shop? ▪ 4

Basement, Garage, or Outbuilding? ▪ 6

Laying Out Your Shop ▪ 14

Shop Floors ▪ 17

Getting Good Light ▪ 19

Using Compressed Air ▪ 23

Controlling Your Shop's Climate ▪ 25

Doors and Other Forms of Egress ▪ 28

Chapter 2
The Clean and Safe Shop ▪ 34

Keeping a Clean Shop ▪ 36

Body Armor ▪ 42

Safety Jigs ▪ 44

Making Machines Safer ▪ 47

Chapter 3
Clever Workstations ▪ 52

Work Supports ▪ 54

Auxiliary Tables ▪ 69

Mobile Workstations ▪ 73

Multipurpose Setups ▪ 75

Sharpening Stations ▪ 77

Sanding Centers ▪ 80

Vacuum Veneering Setups ▪ 84

Finishing Areas ▪ 86

Chapter 4
Storage Solutions · 90

Stashing Wood · 92

Storing Tools · 108

Clamping Gear · 138

Hardware and Supplies · 143

Sanding and Finishing Supplies · 149

Chapter 5
Benches and Worktables · 152

Workbenches · 154

Assembly Tables · 163

Resources · 166

Credits · 169

Introduction

The workshop is an evolving space. Even when fitted with the best of tools, supplies, and setups, it still requires attention as your needs and skills develop. That's where this book comes in. It's filled with all sorts of clever ideas that will help you improve your shop. Whether you're new to the craft or a lifelong, grizzled veteran, there are solutions here for every type of woodworker and for practically every aspect of woodworking. From shop layout strategies and important safety systems to smart tool and workstation assemblies, handy storage schemes, and innovative benches and worktables, you're sure to find ideas that not only improve your shop but also make your woodworking more rewarding.

I've organized this book into chapters that let you incorporate new ideas in a logical and sequential manner. For example, the first chapter starts with basic shop layout and discusses the pros and cons of different types of shops. If you're just starting out, use this section as a guide for equipping your space with all the essentials to build a solid foundation on which to grow a great shop. On the flip side, if you've been in your shop for a while and are simply looking for some inspiration, you can use the ideas in this section to fill in the gaps or to revamp some of your existing systems to make them even better.

The following chapter presents strategies for keeping the shop clean and for making it a safer working environment. While having a tidy shop nears the top of most woodworkers' wish lists, corralling and containing shop sawdust is a priority for everyone in terms of safeguarding one's health. In addition to these dust-busting schemes, you'll find specific safety precautions and setups that make machine work—and your shop in general—much friendlier and safer.

Workstations are covered next, from work holders, such as sawhorses and clamping gear, to tool supports for the table saw, bandsaw, drill press, and other essential machines. Mobile and multipurpose stations that increase your shop's versatility

▲ A ROOM WITH A VIEW. Your workspace will quickly become a favored spot if you let in natural light and provide good bench and storage space. Built-in counters below tall windows offer a great place to work as well as store tools and supplies.

are included. If you want better work flow, easier stock management, and quality cuts, here's the place to look. There are also ingenious ideas for adding or fine-tuning other important work areas, including better sharpening, sanding, veneering, and finishing arrangements.

Keeping track of everything you've got is only possible if you incorporate intelligent storage schemes into the shop. In this next section, you'll discover ways to stack and store lumber so you can access it without having to pull apart an entire pile. Well-thought-out tool storage is discussed, with dozens of ideas for keeping your prized hand tools and accessories neatly organized and within easy reach. Places for clamps and clamping gear are also offered, allowing you to acquire a decent collection while making it serenely accessible during those frantic glue-ups. There are even novel designs for stashing hardware, so you can stock all the myriad fasteners and furniture hardware that the crafting of wooden things demands. Storing sanding and finishing supplies makes up the final part of this section, letting you stockpile your gear in a logical manner so your work flows as smoothly and reliably as your last coat of finish.

Finally, every shop needs a decent bench. This last section not only provides some solid options in this area but also shows you ways of creating additional worksurfaces, with work counters and special-purpose benches that let you tackle a broader range

▲ WORK WHERE YOU'RE COMFORTABLE. **Setting up a table saw in front of a garage door allows easy access, good light, and a cool breeze during hot weather. Building support tables around the saw increases its versatility and lets you saw and stack parts with less effort.**

of woodworking. You'll even find worktables that make final assembly easier, so all your careful machine and benchwork comes together in a harmonious and peaceful whole.

So get ready to dig into a shopful of inspiring ideas, gathered from woodworking shops all over the country. Some are original; some are borrowed from centuries-old ideas and incorporated into today's modern woodshop. All have the unique trait of making your shop the best it can be.

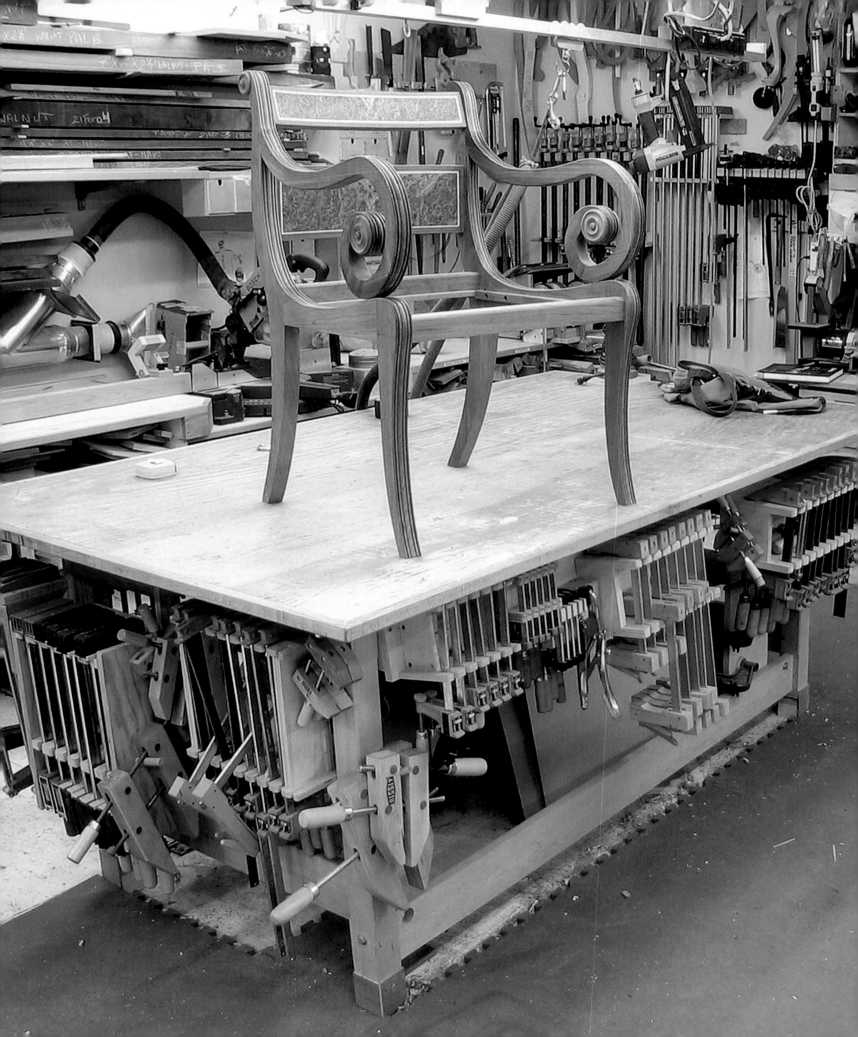

What Makes a Good Shop?

All woodworkers dream of the ideal shop, but it's different for each woodworker. Period furniture makers use a lot of hand tools and need to keep them sorted and accessible, while cabinetmakers require a lot of space. Hobbyists can often make do with smaller tools that take up less room, whereas professionals want big, space-hungry machines. But all great shops have some things in common: tools and work areas laid out in a logical manner, a decent floor, good light to work by, compressed air, a comfortably warm—or cool—working space, and decent access for you and your work through doors and other passageways. With these essentials, you're on your way to having the shop of your dreams.

This chapter explores these key shop components and how you can incorporate them into your own workspace. The first step is to take a good look at the type of shop you're currently in—or hope to be in. You may find that working in the basement, where family and friends drop by without warning, isn't your cup of tea. Perhaps you'd be better off in a separate space where there are fewer disruptions, such as a building located away from home. Maybe the reverse is true: You enjoy the convenience and accessibility of working out of the house, and a recently cleared-out garage space beckons. Once you've found your spot, get ready to pull out the stops to make your shop the ultimate place to hang out...oh, and to work in, too!

◄ A COMFORTABLE PLACE TO WORK. **A great shop starts with the essentials: strong light and fresh air, clean and comfortable floors, organized tools and supplies, and plenty of bench space with room to move around.**

Basement, Garage, or Outbuilding?

OTHER THAN COMMANDEERING THE ATTIC or a spare bedroom, there are three primary spaces to work wood: in the basement, in an attached garage, or in a detached shop, such as an outbuilding on your property or away from home. Each location has its advantages and disadvantages.

The first order of business in any of these shops is to address their particular shortcomings to make them more workable. Basements typically need better light, upgraded wiring, and perhaps heat. Walls and ceilings can be insulated against drafts and to contain dust and noise.

If the garage shares space with a car to two, you can place gear against walls and mobilize your freestanding machines so you can move them when necessary. Large, purpose-built shops will tax your wallet in construction costs, but the expense can be offset if you build furniture for a living.

▶ THE ULTIMATE SHOP? **The modern barnlike shop at Four Sisters Woodworking in Northern California is large, open, and filled with lots of natural and artificial light. A dream shop, the building accommodates two professionals who designed it expressly for woodworking.**

▶ CRAMPED BUT COZY. **Small spaces, such as this basement workshop, can be comfortably intimate as long as you organize your supplies and arrange tools in a logical order, making everything readily accessible so work flows smoothly.**

Pros and Cons of Three Types of Shops

BASEMENT

PROS

- Readily available
- Cool in the summer and can be warmed with your home's heating system during colder months

CONS

- While easy to get to, access can be a problem if the only way out for large workpieces is up a stairway
- Typically suffers from poor light
- Working space can be limited, including low ceilings
- Noise can irritate family members above
- Visiting friends and family can be a distraction

GARAGE

PROS

- Readily available
- Airy room already outfitted with large, overhead doors

CONS

- Sharing space with cars and standing on a cold, concrete slab in the winter can get uncomfortable
- Can get hot in warm months
- Noise can irritate family members through walls and doors
- Visiting friends and family can be a distraction

OUTBUILDING

PROS

- Size can be cozy and intimate or big and industrial
- Lots of natural light
- Keeps you away from the distractions at home
- You can buy, build, or rent

CONS

- Cost: You'll have to fork over monthly utility costs, and construction can drain resources

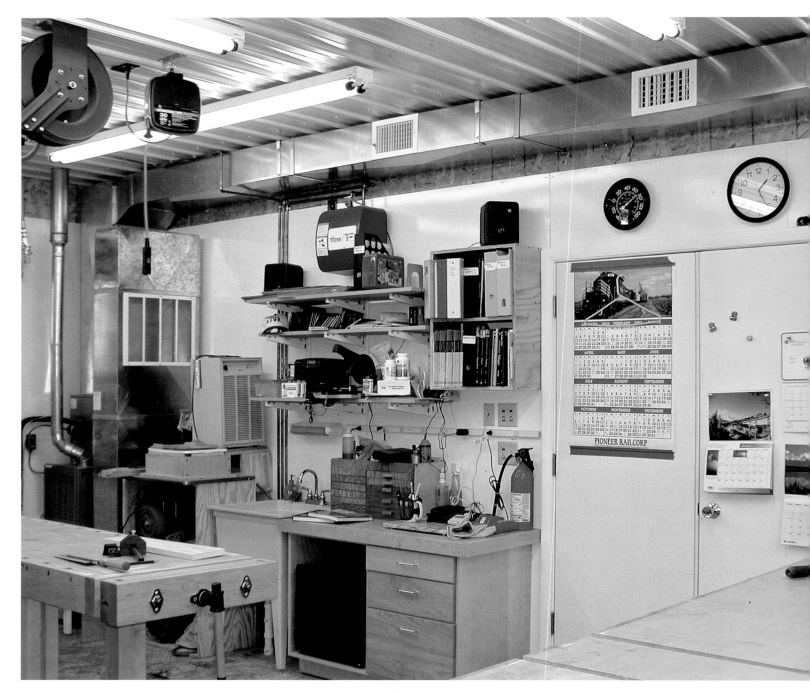

▲ WHITE IS LIGHT. To brighten the workspace, Spence DePauw hung glossy, white metal roofing on the ceiling to bounce light downward and added 1/8-in. sheets of white, melamine-covered hardboard over existing walls. Bonus: He jots down notes anywhere he wants using dry-erase markers.

▲ NATURAL LIGHT BEATS ARTIFICIAL LIGHT HANDS DOWN. If your basement is partially aboveground, you can incorporate windows on the exposed walls. If not, add plenty of artificial light from incandescent and fluorescent fixtures.

Dedicated Shop Power

IF YOU WORK AT HOME IN THE BASEMENT OR GARAGE, you'll need to find a way to get sufficient power to your machines, especially if some of them require 220 volts or more. One approach is to have the electric company install a new line to the house. An easier method, particularly if you have a 200-amp service, typical of most modern homes, is to branch off your house's electric panel and mount a separate panel in your workspace. For most shops, 100 amps is sufficient. Make sure to use suitably sized breakers for specific machines, and label them so you can easily disconnect power for maintenance.

▲ GLASS DOORS ARE IDEAL for letting in light, and a screen filters in fresh air. More importantly, walkout doors make it easier to get supplies in and carry large workpieces out. But you'll only find them on basements that have at least one wall aboveground.

◄ FORGET THE CARS. A detached garage has the benefits of a separate out-building, and sometimes you can find a house with one already on the property, so you won't have to build a shop.

▼ ONCE YOU DEAL WITH THE CAR ISSUE, a garage shop can make a nice space with its heavy-duty floor, high ceilings, and large overhead doors. Pull-down stairs can provide access for additional storage, keeping clutter to a minimum.

Restraining the Roar

HOME SHOPS CAN DRIVE FAMILY MEMBERS TO DISTRACTION with their power-tool whistle, whine, and buzz. To tame the noise from your machines, you can mount 1 in. or thicker rigid-foam panels over top of or between rafters on ceilings, between studs in walls, and even on doors. The panels will lower noise levels while deadening vibrations, which can be just as annoying. To really cut down on the racket, consider installing a drop-down ceiling (in a basement) using acoustic ceiling tiles. Then build subwalls around the shop, leaving an air space of 1 in. to 2 in. between the existing walls and the new ones, where noise and vibration fall short before entering the house.

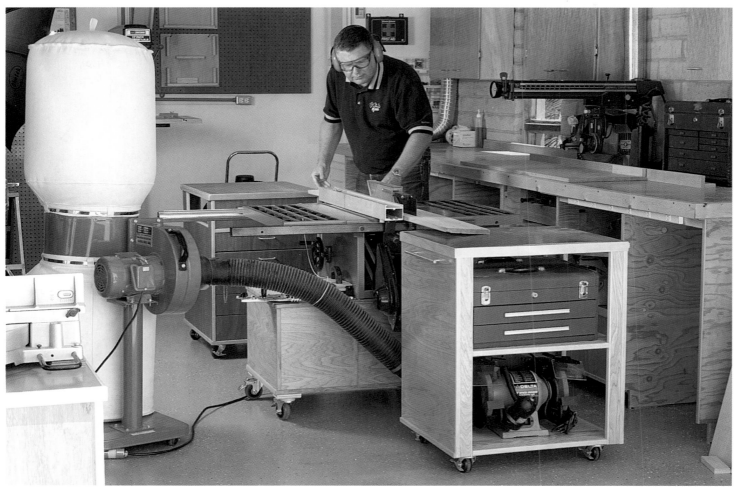

▲ ▼ MAKE ROOM FOR CARS AND TOOLS.
Plywood boxes with casters let you
create a roll-away workshop. Calculate
the height of the boxes so they function as tool bases and feed tables, and
incorporate space under counters for
stowing them out of the way at the
end of the day.

OUTBUILDING: THE DREAM SHOP

◀ LOCATION, LOCATION, LOCATION. Large glass windows and a streetside location can announce your business and draw in customers. Instead of just a showroom, chair-maker Don Weber has his workshop on the main street so passersby can see the action inside.

▼ A NICE ADDITION. A 600-ft. to 700-ft. single-story building in your backyard is big enough for making furniture without overwhelming the neighborhood. So the build-ing doesn't look out of place, tie the siding, trim, and colors to those on your house.

▶ A FAMILY COMPOUND. The Nakashima Workshops, a family-run business, consists of multiple woodworking-related buildings all nestled on the same property. Each serves a specific function, such as storage sheds, a cabinet shop, a chair shop, a finishing shop, and a gallery of work. Path-ways lead from one shop to the other.

▲ TAILOR THE SHOP TO YOUR WORK. **If you do mostly hand-tool work and don't need the space that power tools require, then a small, rustic shop like chairmaker Curtis Buchanan's can work for you. Going small and economical means you can add touches like a porch, which makes a great spot for working outdoors in the shade.**

► AWAY FROM HOME. **You can usually find affordable space to buy, rent, or lease downtown. Old service garages are good candidates, with sufficient electrical service, solid floors, great access, and plenty of parking. Let the old signage remain if you're not actively seeking woodworking visitors.**

Laying Out Your Shop

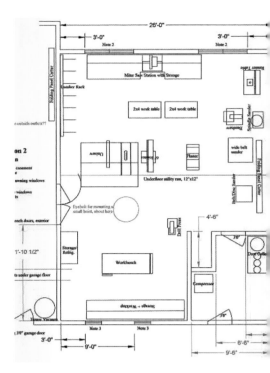

PLACING ALL THE MAJOR FIXTURES IN YOUR SHOP, from machines, workstations, and benches to storage cabinets and finishing setups, is key to making an efficient working space.

The first step is to decide how everything will fit before you move a single tool. You can use a computer-aided design (CAD) program to produce a detailed plan, or you can fashion a scaled plan from scrap plywood or paper that lets you move miniature tools around without breaking a sweat.

Arrange your tools and work areas by concentrating on the work flow, creating a natural movement for you and your wood from one workstation to the next. Also, determine how much space a particular tool needs to function. Some tools, such as the table saw, require large, open areas around them. Others can be tucked against a wall or into a niche and still perform well.

▲ LAYOUT HELP. You can lay out your shop by making a scaled drawing on the computer. There are many affordable and user-friendly software programs that allow you to draw your workspace to scale, including its dimensions and the machines that will go in it. Some are free for downloading off the Internet.

▲ WORK AROUND THE BENCH. Similar to the efficient work triangle of kitchens, the bench area should stock everything you need in a relatively small area. Even if the workbench commands center stage, it should be supported by additional work counters with tools and supplies nearby.

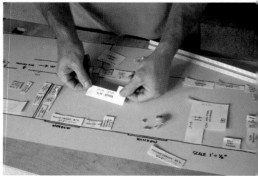

▲ THE OLD-FASHIONED WAY. Using an architect's rule, you can create paper scale models of all your gear and the space they occupy. Photographer's "blue tack" holds cutouts in place. Rearrange the paper tools as many times as you like—without ever muscling heavy cast iron.

▲ GO IN ORDER. If possible, place wood storage near an entrance. Then arrange your machines in the order they'll be used, from pulling rough lumber off the rack for crosscutting to milling on the jointer, planer, and table saw and then shaping on the router table or shaper.

▲ SOME TOOLS ARE SPACE HOGS. The table saw tops the list and can use as much as 16 ft. in front of and behind the blade and at least 8 ft. to one side. Other machines, such as jointers and planers, need sufficient infeed and outfeed room.

Positioning Electrical Outlets

WHEN WIRING YOUR SHOP, locate the electrical outlets and phone jacks about 50 in. above the floor (if your local building codes allow). That way, they don't get covered if you lean a sheet of plywood against the wall. The raised receptacles will also allow easy access to power or phone if you place your workbench under them.

▼ DIVIDE THE SPACE. **Accessible but separate, the bench area is isolated from the machine room with a solid wall. This allows you to concentrate on refinements such as joinery, smoothing work, and assembly in a calm, quiet, and clean area.**

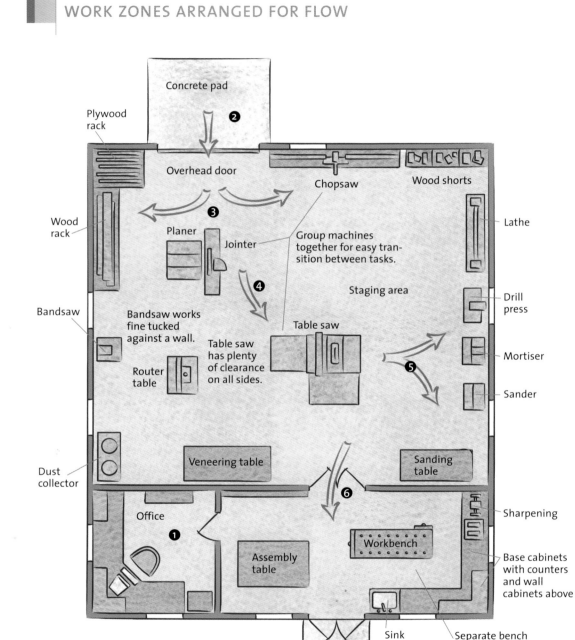

Concrete pad

❷

Plywood rack

Overhead door

Chopsaw

Wood shorts

❸

Wood rack

Planer

Jointer

Group machines together for easy transition between tasks.

Lathe

Staging area

❹

Bandsaw

Bandsaw works fine tucked against a wall.

Table saw has plenty of clearance on all sides.

Table saw

Drill press

Router table

Mortiser

❺

Sander

Dust collector

Veneering table

Sanding table

❻

Office

Sharpening

❶

Workbench

Assembly table

Base cabinets with counters and wall cabinets above

Sink

Separate bench area from machines to reduce dust and noise.

❼

❶ Design and planning
❷ Material delivery
❸ Rough stock prep
❹ Milling
❺ Shaping
❻ Joinery, assembly, finishing
❼ Out the door

Shop Floors

STAND ON COLD CONCRETE FOR MORE THAN AN HOUR, and your feet and back—plus the occasional dropped tool—will soon appreciate the joy of a more forgiving shop floor. Wood is the ideal stepping surface because it's resilient, providing a cushioned surface. Properly braced, it can support as much load as you want. However, not all of us have the luxury of solid-wood floors. Luckily, there are some alternatives.

The easiest approach is to place a soft material over your hard floor. Rubber mats and carpet provide good support, protect tools, insulate from cold, and deaden sound and vibration. The same is true if you lay sheets of plywood over concrete. Although it's more work, it's a great way to insulate while providing the feel of wood under your feet.

▲ VACUUM, DON'T SWEEP. Carpet with thick padding underneath is a viable and back-saving alternative, especially at the bench where you stand for many hours. The catch? You'll have to grab the shop vacuum to suck up shavings and other debris that clings to carpet fibers.

▲ WOOD FEELS GOOD. A solid-wood strip floor is comfortable because it flexes enough to keep your legs and back from tiring during long standing stints. Since it's wood, you can saw or rout into it to run power lines so they lie flush with the floor.

▲ STRONG ENOUGH FOR HEAVY IRON. Hardwood flooring can handle plenty of weight as long as it's properly supported by floor joists below. Look for dense, tropical species being imported as flooring, which compete favorably in price with domestic materials.

◀ PADDING WHERE YOU NEED IT. Cushioned mats lessen fatigue and come in an astounding variety of shapes, sizes, and colors. You can tailor-fit them around workstations, from workbenches and sharpening areas to table saws, bandsaws, and other machines. A textured surface provides good grip.

Getting Good Light

GOOD LIGHT IS OFTEN AN OVERLOOKED ASPECT of creating a great shop. Sure, you can plug in as many spotlights as you need and install rows of fluorescent fixtures overhead, but you still may be working in poor light.

The best light is natural daylight, so take advantage of windows, skylights, and glass doors where you can. The next best bet is incandescent or halogen lights, or any light that emits a strong beam of luminosity. These light sources, as well as natural light, throw shadows. Shadows create good contrast, which helps define objects and gives them dimension.

While fluorescent lights are desirable for brightening an entire room, they cast almost no shadow and create a bland, flat effect, making it difficult to pick out details, such as when carving or finishing. The best solution is to use as many types of light as possible for a range of illumination.

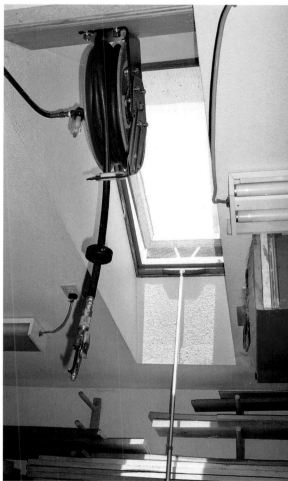

◀ ▲ SUNLIGHT IS BEST. **Natural light from windows, doors, and skylights is your best bet for seeing clearly in the shop. Well-placed skylights can brighten an entire room and add ventilation if they're operable. Position tools and workstations under windows, and use blinds if the sun shines directly in.**

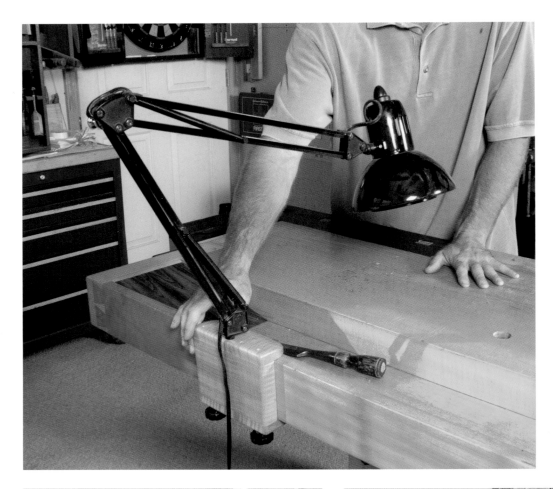

◄ MOVABLE LIGHT. This shopmade task-light holder lets you move the fixture anywhere along the back rail of your bench. The two-piece holder bolts together and has top and bottom lips that grab the rail to prevent the fixture from tipping.

▼ DETAIL WORK NEEDS THE RIGHT LIGHT. Incandescent, articulating task lights are perfect for the bench, where you need to see details up close. For benches with dog holes, drill a hole in a piece of scrap wood for the light's post, and then pop the assembly into the most convenient dog hole. You can also get a fixture with a clamp.

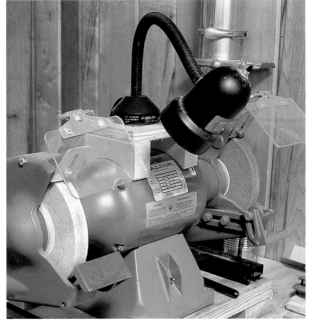

▲ NOT JUST FOR THE OFFICE. Illuminate your work, such as when grinding, by bolting a standard desk-style task light to a wooden support. Shape the support so it fits the contours of the tool, and then secure it with construction adhesive or double-sided tape.

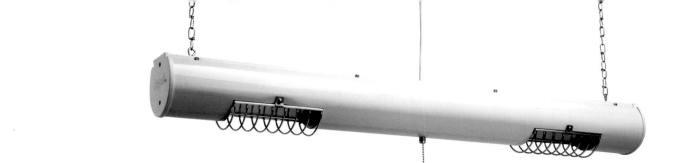

▲ CHOOSE THE LEVEL OF LIGHT. This halogen fixture throws out plenty of diffused light through glass covers, brightening any area and providing good contrast. A pull cord lets you choose between 300 or 600 watts so you can increase or decrease output on the fly.

◄ BE INNOVATIVE. Placing your workbench near a window lets you see details with clarity. Open tool racks mounted across the window keep hand tools accessible without blocking light.

► YOU DON'T NEED SOMETHING FANCY. Tube-style fluorescent fixtures are inexpensive to install and run and will brighten everything in the room. The drawback is a very flat light that doesn't show contrast very well. Always back them up with other light sources.

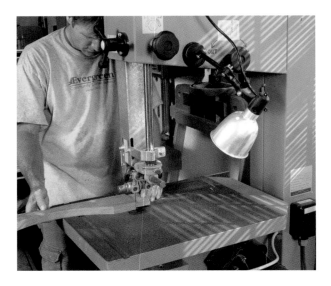

▶ TAKE IT ANYWHERE. This task light has a magnetic base that lets you mount it to any ferrous surface, such as to the steel frame of a bandsaw. An articulating head and arm let you adjust the light precisely where you need it.

ROLL-AROUND SPOTLIGHT

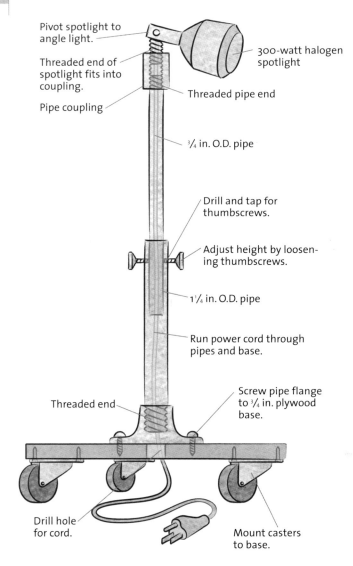

Pivot spotlight to angle light.

Threaded end of spotlight fits into coupling.

Pipe coupling

300-watt halogen spotlight

Threaded pipe end

$\frac{3}{4}$ in. O.D. pipe

Drill and tap for thumbscrews.

Adjust height by loosening thumbscrews.

$1\frac{1}{4}$ in. O.D. pipe

Run power cord through pipes and base.

Screw pipe flange to $\frac{3}{4}$ in. plywood base.

Threaded end

Drill hole for cord.

Mount casters to base.

▲ WHEELS MAKE IT EASY. For superstrong, directional light anywhere you need it in the shop—at any height—make a roll-around, adjustable-height fixture with a 300-watt halogen spotlight mounted on top. Cut the pipe sections so the fixture adjusts to the maximum height you'll need.

Using Compressed Air

HAVING COMPRESSED AIR IN THE SHOP allows you to run a host of pneumatic woodworking tools, from drills and nail guns to sanders, spray guns, and routers—not to mention you can pump up a flat on your car or blow off the day's dust to keep you and your shop tidy. You'll need a compressor, but relax. It doesn't have to be the big beast you see at your local service station.

Check out how much cubic feet per minute (cfm) your tools will need, then find the equivalent rating on the compressor as well as its horse-power (hp) output and tank size. Small portable units can easily fire nail guns or run light-duty tools. Midsized compressors will power high-volume, low-pressure (HVLP) spray guns and can still be portable if on wheels. For serious work, large, fixed-based units can run sanders or conventional spray equipment all day long.

▲ PORTABLE NAILER. A small compressor can power one or two nail guns all day long. Its relative light weight lets you use it in the workshop, or carry it around the house or to the job site for trimwork or installations.

▲ MIDSIZED SPRAYER. A midsized compressor like this 25-gal. unit can handle all sorts of jobs, including light sanding and spraying with a low-pressure gun. Wheels and a handle let you move it from spot to spot, but don't expect to get it up the stairs.

▲ SAND ALL DAY. A large compressor won't need to run continuously even when supplying air-hungry tools such as standard spray guns or sanders. This 60-gal. unit produces about 10 cfm of air at 90 pounds per square inch (psi), and will let you spray or sand all day.

◄ AIR ON HIGH. Big compressors are noisy and take up precious real estate. To move the noise upward and reclaim some floor space, consider installing your unit on a high shelf. Tie into framing members in the wall or ceiling to support the weight.

Controlling Your Shop's Climate

KEEPING A SHOP WARM OR COOL IS A CONCERN if the space you work in has no climate control. In a basement shop, cooling is probably not an issue. In hot garages and outbuildings, you can open doors and windows and use fans to cool off. Fortunately, there are many heating options, from extending your home's oil- or gas-fired furnace to installing woodstoves, gas, and radiant-heat arrangements.

Another key climate issue is your shop's humidity level, which should remain as constant as possible. If the air is too dry, your wood will shrink and possibly crack and distort. Pans of water placed in front of fans can add moisture back into the air. If the shop becomes humid, you'll be sweltering, your finishes will misbehave, and again, your wood will suffer—this time by swelling. The most effective approach is to monitor moisture with a humidity gauge, and invest in a dehumidifier for those really wet days.

◀ ▲ PICK YOUR GAS. You can choose a sealed-flame heater that runs on propane, natural gas, or kerosene. Most require venting to the outside. Slim units like the propane heater shown at left can be mounted on a wall. Others, like the natural gas heater shown above, hang unobtrusively from the ceiling and are vented through the roof.

◀ WOOD IS GOOD. Burning wood sounds risky, but many woodworkers use this simple heating system very effectively and are happy to use shop scraps as part of their fuel. Be sure to surround the stove with heat-resistant material, and keep a tidy shop.

▼ HEAT FROM ABOVE. Radiant heat warms people and objects first, keeping you and your materials warm while the surrounding air can be cooler. One system employs a series of thin, 4x8 ceiling-mounted panels that run on electricity and are safe enough to use in a finish room.

▶ HEAT FROM BELOW. A radiant floor system has hot-water pipes under the floor that keep an entire shop warm, not just your feet. Installation is more involved, since you have to install piping under the floor. The system here works off a standard oil-fired water heater.

◀ DRY AIR IS BETTER. When the shop becomes humid, try circulating the air with fans to dry it out. When that fails, invest in a dehumidifier. Small, portable units are best placed in a central spot. You can hook up a dedicated drain line, or empty the unit manually when it's full.

◀ ▲ SAFETY FIRST. Dust can be a real problem for conventional furnace-type heaters. To address the issue before it reaches your system, install double filters in all air-intake vents. Be sure to inspect filters regularly and clean or replace them as necessary.

Doors and Other Forms of Egress

MOVING YOU AND YOUR WORK throughout the shop takes some careful planning. By providing good access via doors and other ways of moving about, your work can flow smoothly around the shop and eventually move safely out the door.

Inside, think about the work flow when locating doors and other access points, including which way a door should open. If dust is a problem, make sure to close off sensitive areas, such as offices filled with computer equipment and finishing rooms. To move really big stuff, such as machines or heavy materials, carts and dollies can sometimes fall short. Consider equipping your shop with a hoist, which saves your back and can carry monster loads.

Exterior doors should be situated so people as well as vehicles can get to them. Providing a hard surface outside an entranceway, such as a concrete pad, makes for easy loading and unloading.

▶ SAFE AND WIDE. Double doors let you move large loads without hassle. Insulated, steel doors are workshop-tough and provide sound deadening as well as fire protection.

▲ ▶ EASY IN AND OUT. Large exterior doors on barn-door tracks slide open to make awkward loads more manageable, and glass panes keep the shop well lit. Inside, another set of doors separates wood storage from the main shop.

▼ ▶ KEEP IT QUIET. The entrance to Rob Porcaro's basement shop looks like any normal home passageway (below). But inside, the doors are lined with acoustic ceiling tile attached with construction adhesive. This effectively reduces the spread of machine noise throughout the rest of the house.

◄ INDUSTRIAL SHOP DIVIDER. An interior garage door makes sense for large shops, separating workspaces and providing ample passage for moving big stuff. This plastic-paneled door keeps spaces well lit and lets you see what's coming— a real boon in a busy shop.

▲ FIT THE DOOR TO THE SPACE. Paired doors lead into the finishing room at Placeways Woodworking, keeping out shop dust. The glazed door on the right lets in light and allows the worker to see who's coming. On the left is a recycled screen door that's been fitted with filters to provide clean airflow.

◄ PROTECT YOUR PAPERWORK IN STYLE. Cabinetmaker Frank Klausz's paired doors keep dust and dirt from migrating into the shop office. For fun, he used a variety of wood species for the doors and trim. Even the mullions are individual woods, with color-matched putty behind them to hold the glass.

▲ MODIFIED GARAGE DOOR. A standard garage door adapted to lift upward saves room overhead so there's space for moving tall boards and gear. Furniture maker Joe Tracy sawed kerfs in the door tracks and then straightened them, allowing the door to open almost vertically. Counterweights make it easy to raise.

▶ BIGGER CAN BE BETTER. Large garage doors can really open up a building, allowing easy access for large gear and even vehicles. A row of windows at head height lets you see out or in and spreads natural light into the shop.

▼ LET IN THE LIGHT. A glazed door is perfect for dark shops, letting in light and announcing visitors at the same time. To keep you and your work dry, place an awning over the entrance to ward off the weather.

Getting Heavy Loads Inside

T SOME POINT, most woodworkers face moving a really heavy load into or out of the shop, such as a large cabinet, a monster plank of wood, or a newly purchased machine. Without the aid of a helper, the job can be daunting. A chain hoist can solve the problem and gives you the ability to move really big stuff all by yourself.

For this system to work well, keep a few things in mind. Make sure the hoist is rated for the load you need to lift, and mount it securely to a beam or joist that has sufficient load-carrying strength. Steel I-beams are ideal, but heavy wood joists work well, too. Choose the hoist's location carefully. A central beam in the shop, near an exterior loading door, is preferable. This way, you can haul in stuff safely without hitting an opening or getting it stuck midway through a door.

▲ HEAVY-DUTY HOIST. With a heavy-duty hoist and proper strapping, it's a one-person affair to lift and maneuver heavy supplies or gear, such as this production jointer.

▼ CHAIN HOIST. Situated in the center of the room near the entrance and the lumber rack, this chain hoist rides overhead on a steel beam mounted to the ceiling.

2

The Clean and Safe Shop

Playing it safe in the shop is no accident. Using the right gear and equipping your machines and tools with proper safety devices and decent dust collection will make your shop a comfortable, safe place to do woodworking.

A clean shop is smart for your health and reduces the chance of accidents. Good dust collection is the key, and there are many solutions offered here. It's also wise to protect yourself by donning safety eyewear, hearing protection, and masks to keep eyes and ears safe and lungs clean and healthy.

Jigs are another important part of a woodworker's safety arsenal. They guide a tool or workpiece in a controlled manner so you don't have any mishaps. The same is true of your machines: Setting them up correctly and arming them with good safety equipment will boost your confidence level and make your milling operations safer and more accurate.

Remember to use common sense in your shop, and be alert to potential problems. If something doesn't feel right to you, stop and check it out before picking up a tool or switching on a machine. Your instincts are probably right. There is always a safe way to do woodworking.

◄ A SAFE WAY TO WORK. Ear and eye protection is only the tip of the iceberg when it comes to working without risk to yourself or your work. Safe machining, such as table saw work, includes dust collection, guards, hold-ins, push sticks, and splitters.

Keeping a Clean Shop

NOT ONLY IS A CLEAN SHOP MORE PLEASURABLE TO WORK IN, but it's also safer. While storing tools and supplies is half the battle, you still have to deal with the huge amounts of dust, chips, and dirt you generate on a daily basis. Ongoing strategies for cleaning up this mess are a must if you want to keep a clear head and a clean bench.

There are several approaches you can take to keep a tidy shop. One is to clean daily by sweeping and vacuuming up debris. The other is to install a dust-collection system to capture chips and dust from the machines that generate them. But dust collectors can't trap all the fine particles. Thankfully, there are other cleaning tactics that help fend off the mess. (See Sanding Centers, pp. 80–83, for sanding solutions.)

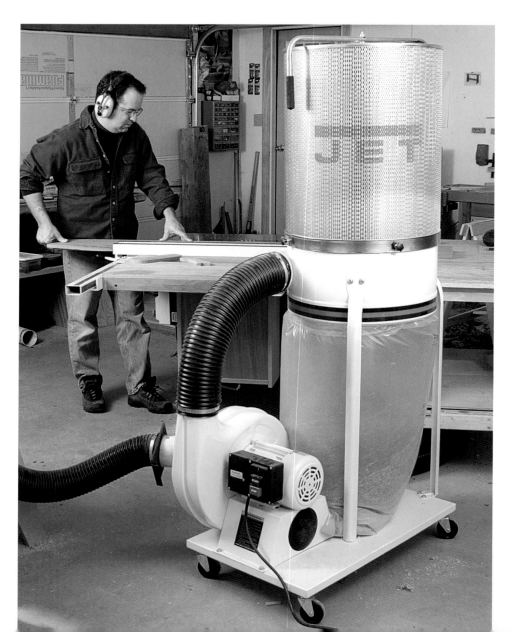

► CATCH IT AT THE SOURCE. Dust collectors are a major step up from vacuums and can be hooked to a dedicated pipeline that feeds all the major machines in the shop. Newer models have cartridge-based filters that capture superfine particles as well as chips.

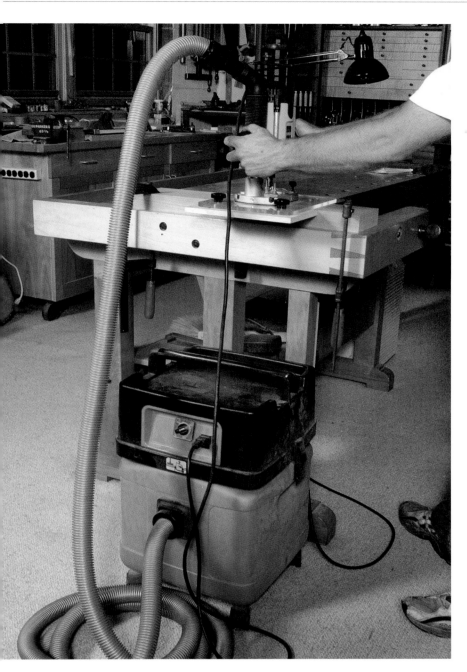

▲ SEE WHAT YOU GET. The lower bags on dust collectors gather the waste and require regular emptying. To make the job fool-proof, look for clear bags or bags with windows that tell you when it's time to dump.

▲ AUTOMATIC ON. Some shop vacuums have a special switch that allows you to plug in dust-choking power tools, such as a router. Switch on the tool, and the vacuum springs to life. When you turn the tool off, the vacuum turns off, too.

▶ PUSH, DON'T PULL. A push broom works much better than the standard kitchen sweeper for collecting large piles of debris on smooth shop floors. Move the broom slowly or you'll raise dust clouds, and push it—don't pull—for more control.

DUST-BUSTING STRATEGIES

◄ CLOSE IT UP. Contractor saws are notorious for spewing dust from their open undersides. This commercial dust bag attaches and detaches in minutes, letting you capture chips and haul them off to the trash without having to sweep up.

► A BIG MOUTH IS BETTER. Standard ports can choke on big dust- and chip-spewing machines such as sanders and lathes and don't allow for flexible placement. To trap debris, buy a large, metal dust shroud, attach it to a workstand, and position it to catch the mess.

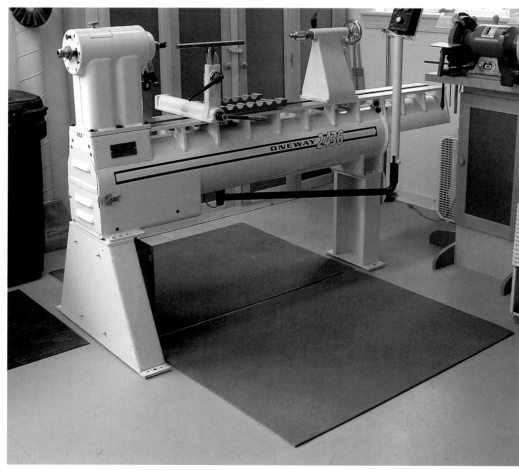

◄ TOUGH AND SLICK. You can improve a concrete floor by covering it with epoxy paint, a durable and extremely long-lasting coating. The epoxy seals the surface and makes it so smooth that dust slides over the surface, making cleanup a snap.

▲ JUST SMOOTH GLASS. For a traditional look that's a breeze to clean and keep clean, install double-pane windows with internal mullions trapped inside the panes. The smooth surface doesn't trap dust and makes quick wipe-downs much easier.

▲ FLEX TO FIT. Tools such as the router table, lathe, and drill press don't work well with a fixed dust port attached. The fix? Install household dryer-vent hose into your dust-collection system and then bend it to where chips are flying.

▶ SWEEP IT IN. If you run a dust-collection system, drop a vertical pipe equipped with a blastgate to the floor and connect a sheet-metal floor sweep at the end. Close the gate during machining, and open it to sweep floor debris without stooping.

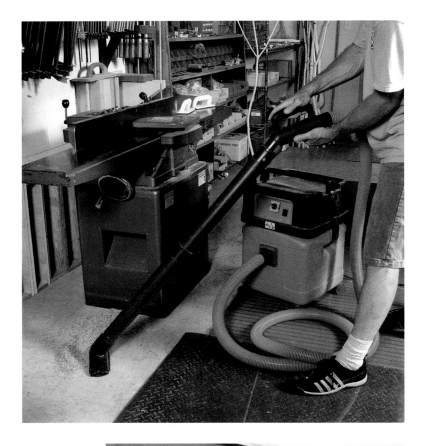

◄ CLEANING HOUSE. In addition to hooking up a shop vacuum to machines, you can use it much like a house vacuum by connecting the hose to a rigid pipe fitted with a floor sweep. Be sure to buy pipe that fits your shop vac's hose diameter.

▲ INSIDE ANOTHER ROOM. You'll reduce shop noise if you locate your collector behind insulated walls. Provide a door for access, and run the main pipe through the wall. Be sure there's makeup air (a filter in the wall works great), or the motor can overheat.

◄ CHIPS AND CLATTER GO OUTSIDE. Large, noisy collectors are best located outdoors, where cleanout is easier. This unit is designed to withstand the weather and is parked adjacent to the shop's wall with pipe running through and to the inside.

◀ FILTER THE AIR. Dust collectors won't catch all dust, especially the tiny (and hazardous) micron-sized particles that can hang in the air for hours. Capture this fine, airborne stuff by hanging an air handler above a sanding area or in a central area in the shop.

▼ IN THE ATTIC. Tired of the noise and wasted space, furniture maker Walt Segl installed his cyclone collector in the crawl space above his shop. A pipe from the cyclone runs to a barrel on the floor below for convenient waste removal.

▲ QUIET AND EASY. A cyclone-type dust collector is quieter than most and separates the chips from the dust, making the operation more efficient and removal of waste much easier. This collector is hooked up to permanent pipes that service machines throughout the shop.

Body Armor

IT PAYS TO PROTECT SENSITIVE AREAS OF YOUR BODY with effective safety gear. A variety of gloves will shield your hands from the rigors of the woodshop. Even more important are your eyes, ears, and lungs. Dust and noise will wreak havoc on your sight, hearing, and respiratory system if you don't take some precautionary measures.

Eyewear is essential, even when using hand tools, which can spit wood splinters or metal particles into your face unexpectedly. For even more protection, consider a full-coverage face shield.

Routers, planers, and chopsaws are some of the worst noise offenders and can cause permanent hearing loss. Wear muffs or ear plugs whenever you plug in a major power tool.

Keep your lungs fit by wearing a dust mask during sanding or heavy machining. For superclean air, consider an air-supplied helmet. If you're exposed to fumes or chemicals, don a cartridge-type respirator.

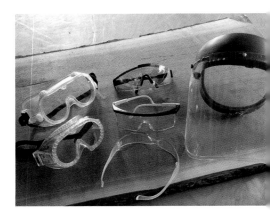

▲ PROTECT YOUR EYES. Glasses should be comfortable (look for adjustable arms) and protect from airborne debris, such as dust or shards of wood. Goggles seal to your face and come in children's sizes. A face shield is great for turning or for protection from other potential flying objects.

◄ STOP DUST AND FUMES. Particle, or nuisance, masks work well to keep small dust particles from entering your lungs (left). For protection against fumes as well as dust, consider a respirator with replaceable cartridges rated for the fumes or chemicals you're working with (right).

▲ BREATHE EASY. This all-in-one, air-supplied helmet protects eyes and lungs from dust and is light-weight and comfortable thanks to its baseball-style cap. A battery-operated motor clipped to your belt (right) delivers clean air even in dusty environments.

▼ LISTEN UP. Ear muffs stop ear-splitting noise and are rated by their maximum allowable decibel level. Disposable plugs block even more noise by conforming to your outer ear without adding weight. Corded models hang conveniently around your neck for frequent removal.

▲ GOOD HANDS. A decent glove selection includes (clockwise from top center): canvas gloves for rough wood handling; heavy rubber gloves to resist chemicals; thin latex gloves for general finishing; Kevlar®-reinforced gloves for protection with maximum dexterity; and welding gloves to deflect heat.

Safety Jigs

A GOOD JIG WILL GUIDE YOUR WORK or the tool you're using so you don't have to rely on brute strength—or luck. There's practically no end to the type of jigs you can buy or build to make your woodworking safer.

How do you know when to use a jig? Ask yourself whether a specific operation feels safe before you attempt to perform it. If it seems at all risky, stop and build—or buy—a jig that helps you get the task done without danger to you or your work. I'll often whip up a jig by nailing together pieces with a nail gun, using glue, plywood, and other shop scrap. The little time it takes to build pays big dividends with better control over the tooling process. As a bonus, many jigs can be used over and over again for several different operations.

▲ STICK WITH FOAM. Push blocks with foam bottoms will grip rough or smooth stock and are especially useful guiding small workpieces, such as on the table saw or router table. Epoxy a magnet flush with the base so you can store the block on a cast-iron machine—right where you'll need it.

▲ GRIP THIS. A commercial router mat made from a cushiony, sticky material will hold medium-sized parts so you can rout freehand without having to set up cumbersome clamps. It also protects work from dings and scratches.

▲ HIGH GETS BY. Make an extra-tall push stick to clear obstructions such as blade guards. Use plywood (and not solid wood) so the heel doesn't split off accidentally as you cut into it. A rounded rear edge makes it comfortable to grip.

▼ STOP SPINNING. V-block jigs are handy on various machines, including the drill press, chopsaw, and bandsaw. Two 45° blocks nailed to a plywood base form a 90° angle, letting you place round or odd-shaped work between them without having the part shift unexpectedly.

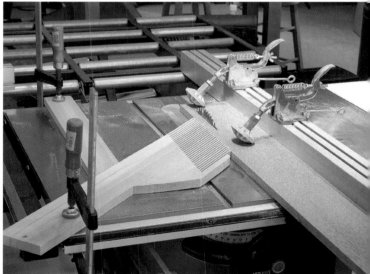

▲ PRESS DOWN AND IN. Commercial hold-downs clamped to fences keep work flat on the table. A featherboard, made from scrap wood with a series of flexible "fingers" cut into one end, places sideways pressure so the work stays safely against the fence.

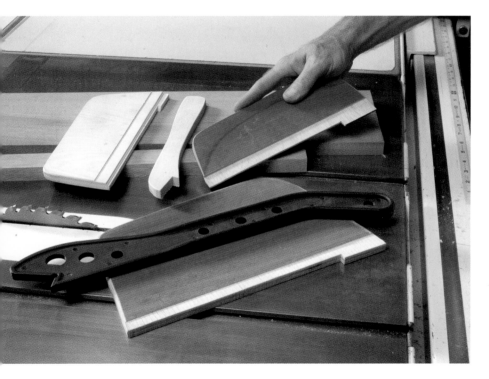

◄ STICKS SAVE FINGERS. Push sticks are handy for all sorts of pushing jobs, and they keep hands clear of the cutting action. You can buy plastic sticks, which can be cut into just like wood, or make your own in various shapes and sizes from shop scraps.

◄ LOOK MA, NO CLAMPS. This commercial magnetic hold-in sticks to any ferrous surface, such as your table saw's tabletop, making it easy to set up. A strip of flexible plastic places pressure against the work so you don't have to.

Handling Small Stock

SOME OF THE MOST POTENTIALLY DANGEROUS OPERATIONS in the shop involve working with small stock, which can move unexpectedly from your grasp during machining. To get a solid grip, consider making a couple of safety aids that hold your work securely.

To move thin strips of wood in narrow spots, an eraser glued to a thin stick of wood will grip without slipping and comes in handy for pushing away offcuts when they're sitting near a spinning bit or blade. Toggle clamps are great finger-savers when it comes to securely holding stock during a cut. You can buy them in various styles and then mount them to jigs so they grasp work while you're busy concentrating on the cut.

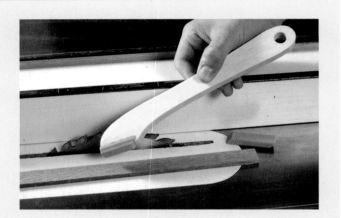

▲ PINPOINT CONTROL. A rubber eraser glued to the end of a thin push stick is just the ticket for gripping supersmall parts. Cut a notch in the plywood stick, then glue the eraser to the notch with epoxy or cyanoacrylate (CA) glue.

► MINI CLAMPS FOR SMALL WORK. You can screw toggle clamps to just about any jig. Here, the clamps provide holding power in a V-block jig designed for cutting round or odd-shaped work. The jig's base is screwed to the fence of the miter gauge.

Making Machines Safer

ALL WOODWORKING TOOLS ARE POTENTIALLY DANGEROUS if you don't take the time to set them up properly. Lubricating working surfaces, such as tables and fences, makes machines safer, since you don't have to fight resistance from accumulated dirt or other sticky stuff. Setting blades and bits to the correct height is another important safety measure.

Guards and splitters are a must if you want to reduce accidents, but the sad truth is that most stock devices are clumsy to set up and use. Luckily, there are some excellent aftermarket versions available, or you can make your own. You can upgrade the on/off switch system on most machines, safeguarding them from curious youngsters and making them easier to use in the bargain. And don't overlook the floor in front of your tools: Get a good grip with your feet so you maintain your balance and feed work with confidence.

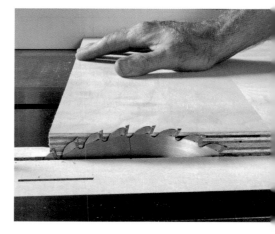

▲ KEEP IT LOW. **Set bit and blade heights so they'll make the cut without exposing more cutter than necessary. On the table saw, raise the blade until the teeth are above the work to provide a clean and safe cut.**

◀ RUB IT IN. **Lubricating your work surfaces with light oil or paste wax keeps rust at bay and makes work glide more easily. To apply wax, rub a generous amount with a rag, then buff it to a shine with cotton cloths until the surface is smooth and slippery.**

GUARDS AND SPLITTERS

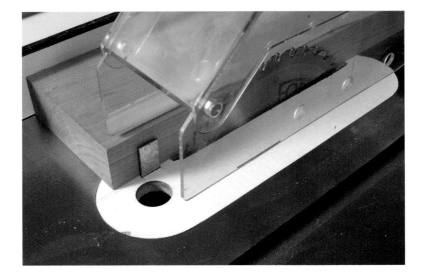

◄ STOP KICKBACK. A splitter, or riving knife, prevents kick-back by keeping stock from engaging the back of the blade. You can make your own from a strip of metal slightly thinner than the blade's teeth, and glue it into a slot cut into the throat plate.

▼ MAKE YOUR OWN COVER. Many woodworkers devise their own shopmade guards for various machines. This acrylic guard mounts to the shaper's stock guard and can be adjusted for various cuts. The clear material keeps fingers safe, while allowing you to see the cutting action.

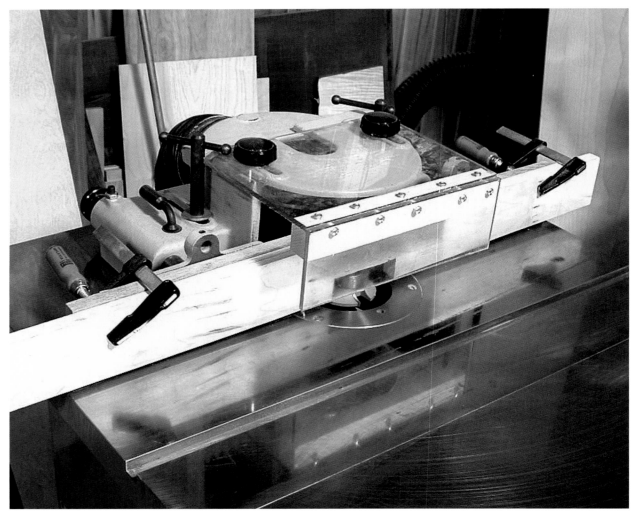

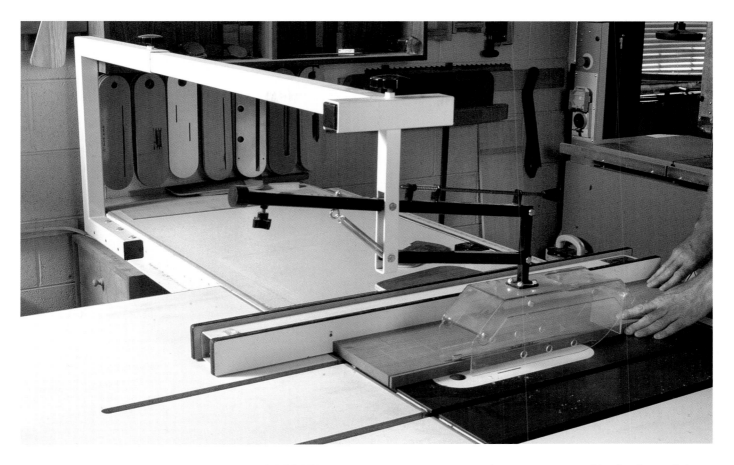

▲ TOOL-FREE REMOVAL. You'll need to routinely remove your splitter when making nonthrough cuts. To make the job hassle-free, this aftermarket splitter locks into a block assembly bolted inside the saw. Simply snap it in place, or remove it with the pull of a knob.

▲ A GUARD YOU'LL USE. There are many user-friendly aftermarket guards available, including this overarm table saw guard that bolts to the sidefeed table. The see-through cover pivots to accommodate thick or thin work and can be easily lifted out of the way or removed entirely for blade changes.

Understanding Kickback

WHEN A BIT OR BLADE GRABS A WORKPIECE **and sends it flying, it's known as kickback. In most cases, the direction the stock moves is backward— at you. Kickback can be caused by dull cutters or by feeding work in the wrong direction. For example, when facing the router table, you should always move stock from left to right past the bit.**

Table saws rank as one of the worst kickback culprits. The single biggest preventative measure you can take is to install a splitter behind the blade. This stops the work from catching on the back of the blade, which is one of the prime causes for kickback.

SWITCHES

▶ OFF WITH A KICK. A wooden stick hinged to the top of the table saw switch kills power with the flick of a foot, letting you keep both hands safely on the workpiece. A hole drilled through the stick lets you engage the power button for turning on the saw.

▼ STOP IT WITH YOUR KNEE. Walt Segl's shopmade crossbar lets him kill power with a knee while standing safely to the left of the blade. The frame bolts to the saw, while a bolt in each support arm allows the bar to pivot into the off switch.

▲ SAFE FROM KIDS. Add this 20-amp switch to any light-duty tool, such as router tables, lathes, and scrollsaws. The large paddle is easy to locate, and a removable insert disengages power so curious hands can't accidentally turn on the machine.

▲ EASY TO PUSH. Mount this 15-amp switch to your router table or other small machine, and access power with ease. The lighted toggle makes turning on your machine a snap, and the large bail lets you turn off power in an instant.

FLOORS THAT GRIP

◄ COAT THE FLOOR WITH SAND AND GLUE. **A quick fix for slippery surfaces is to mix sand with ordinary white or yellow glue, then roll the mixture near the machine you'll be using. The dried-on film provides solid footing right where you need it.**

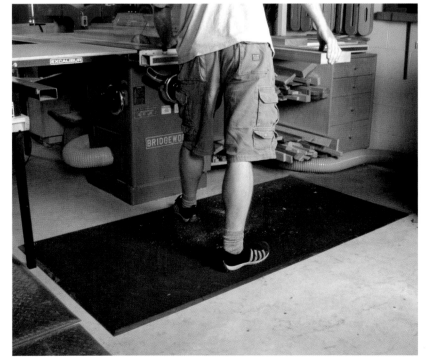

▲ GRIP WITH TAPE. **Apply commercial tape in a mat pattern over slippery wood or concrete floors. Abrasive embedded in the tape keeps your feet solidly planted. If your machine setup changes, simply peel up the old tape and apply a fresh batch where it's needed.**

◄ GOOD FOOTING. **A large, rubber mat in front of your machine gives your feet a good grip and makes feeding stock much safer. Mats with carpet-type "strands" are best because they catch excess chips that could otherwise make the surface area slippery.**

3

Clever Workstations

Buying high-quality woodworking machines and tools is the first step to building a great workshop. But to get the most from your machines, you'll want to add some shopmade accessories and workstations that augment them, increasing their performance, adding versatility, and making cuts more accurate. Keep in mind that machines aren't the only items you can improve. Other work areas, from milling and sanding setups to assembly and finishing systems, can benefit from the same approach as well.

With the right accessories and setups, work flow becomes easier to manage and cuts more precise, with less chance of mistakes on your part. For example, the table saw is much more versatile when outfitted with extension tables that help stock move through the blade more accurately and with less effort. Even a simple clamping arrangement can drastically improve your work and result in glitch-free assemblies. Or perhaps you need to make a few tricky cuts on the router table, but your current setup is awkward or even dangerous. The following workstations address these needs and more, and will help you build a shop full of hardworking tools and setups that will make your woodworking more enjoyable.

◄ SOUPED-UP SAW. **A miter station makes your chopsaw more effective. Paul Anthony's design provides sturdy work support, with fences on either side of the blade to make crosscuts more accurate. A left-side extension increases table length to support extra-long stock, and flip-up stops allow precise, repeat cuts.**

Work Supports

No ONE WOODWORKER OR SINGLE MACHINE CAN DO IT ALL when it comes to handling and processing lumber and sheets of plywood. That's why it makes sense to equip the shop with various "helpers," from tables and rollers that help catch stock as it comes off machines to sawhorses that let you stack stock and special vises that will hold odd or unusual shapes for you while you work.

The table saw is probably the most likely candidate for outfitting with support devices, such as sidefeed and outfeed tables. But don't overlook your smaller tools. The chopsaw, benchtop planer, and even the drill press often benefit from auxiliary surfaces for handling oversize stock. And remember to allocate enough room for all these additions so that large stock, such as 16-ft. boards or full sheets of plywood, can safely make their way around the shop.

▲ MASSIVE CAPACITY. Heavy work requires extra support, and horses made from heavy timbers answer the call. Don Weber used pegged mortise-and-tenon joinery to prevent the horses from racking and to ensure they're up to the task of holding many hundreds of pounds of wood.

◄ JOINTING SUPPORT. With the jointer to the left of the table saw, milling operations are more efficient and support is always on hand for long crosscuts. Instead of using a space-hungry sidefeed table, try clamping a shop-made roller to the bed of the jointer for crosscuts so stock glides smoothly past the blade.

SAWHORSES AND STOOLS

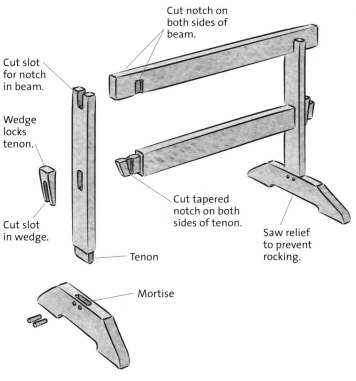

◄ STRONG, LIGHT, AND NESTABLE.
Sawhorses should be strong to
support loads, but they don't
necessarily have to be bulky. The
author's knockdown, trestle-style
horses nest together, can be
made in any height, and a pair
can be carried in one hand and
stored in very little space.

TRESTLE-STYLE SAWHORSE

Cut notch on
both sides of
beam.

Cut slot
for notch
in beam.

Wedge
locks
tenon.

Cut slot
in wedge.

Cut tapered
notch on both
sides of tenon.

Saw relief
to prevent
rocking.

Tenon

Mortise

▲ ▶ UP AND DOWN HORSE. Built-in adjustability lets you work at any height. You can adjust the beam height on Chris Becksvoort's sawhorses by relocating dowels in the drilled uprights. A frame that slides into the horses is capped with a wood dowel wrapped in foam pipe insulation to cushion delicate work.

▲ ▶ USE ALL SIDES. A box-style stool offers maximum versatility since it can be placed on practically any face for a variety of working heights. In standard mode, it makes a sturdy platform for sawing planks and can be used as a low seat when needed. Turned on end, it supports work at the bench with equal aplomb.

SPECIAL CLAMP SETUPS

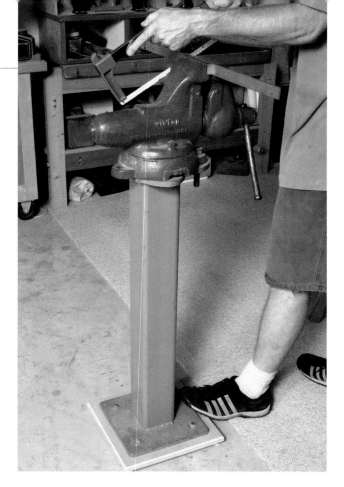

▶ CLAMPING METAL. A standard metalworking vise bolted to heavy metal tubing saves bench space and allows for the occasional metalworking most woodworkers perform. A plywood base mounted to the bottom steadies the vise and allows you to move it when necessary.

▼ ONE VISE FROM TWO. Install two ordinary edge vises along your bench, mount a single wooden jaw across them, and presto! You can now grab long or awkward work without parts slipping. This vise setup is perfect for holding large work, such as long boards or tabletops.

Padding Your Jaws

BOLTING OR SCREWING WOODEN JAWS to standard metal woodworking edge vises is a well-known trick for gripping workpieces without gouging them with hard, metal surfaces. The next step is to line your wood jaws with top-grain cowhide, which provides an even softer cushion while improving the overall grip. For metal-working vises, where the metal jaws are often necessary for securely holding metal parts, try adding removable hardwood blocks. This is sometimes the only way to get a powerful grip on metal parts without scoring or gouging.

▶ LEATHER IS BETTER. Lining wood jaws with leather improves grip and helps protect work so it won't get marred. To apply it, dilute some white or yellow glue with water and coat the back of each piece of leather. Place the pieces between the jaws, and clamp. After the leather dries (and shrinks tight), trim the excess.

▶ WOOD THAT STAYS PUT. Installing removable (and easily replaceable) wood blocks in metalworking vises allows maximum clamp pressure without marring the work. To prevent the jaws from slipping, epoxy some rare-earth magnets flush with the blocks' surface, then stick the blocks to the vise. When you're done, remove the blocks and stick them on the side of the vise so they don't get lost.

▶ SHAVING AROUND. Shaping narrow, long stock in the round is easy if you have a shaving horse. Chairmaker Brian Boggs' shopmade model grips work firmly via a clamping head that he actuates with his foot, leaving his hands free to manipulate tools as he pleases.

◀ CLAMP AND SAW. A traditional French chevalet lets you saw intricate marquetry designs in thin veneer by holding the saw dead square to the work. The thin blade is held in a movable frame, and you use your foot for clamping, allowing you to manipulate the workpiece with one hand as you saw out your design.

MACHINE SUPPORTS

▶ SLIDE-UP SUPPORT. Steadying long work on the drill press is easier if you mount a block to the end of a nearby bench. Lon Schleining attached a support with a hanger bolt and routed a slot so the block can be lowered out of the way when it's not in use.

▼ TWO TOOLS IN ONE. Locating a radial-arm saw and chopsaw in one workstation saves space and lets you use the same fence system for each machine. Make sure the fences on the chopsaw are aligned with the station's fences for accurate crosscuts.

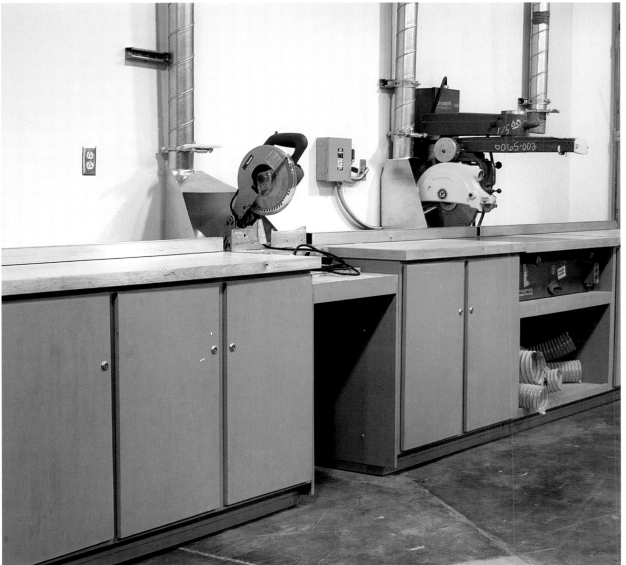

▲ BIG PLANING FROM A SMALL MACHINE.
Gain greater capacity from your benchtop
planer by mounting it to a metal rack
fitted with stock support blocks that
equal the planer's table height. John
McDermott's setup and spacing stabilizes
even long boards and has two shelves
below for stock storage.

◄ INSTANT OUTFEED. You can raise a workbench to catch the ends of long, heavy
boards as they come off the bandsaw,
making sawing more accurate and less
tiring. The ADJUSTABENCH® in Geoffrey
Noden's shop features a range of bench
heights to accommodate various setups,
with locking casters that keep it steady
as you saw.

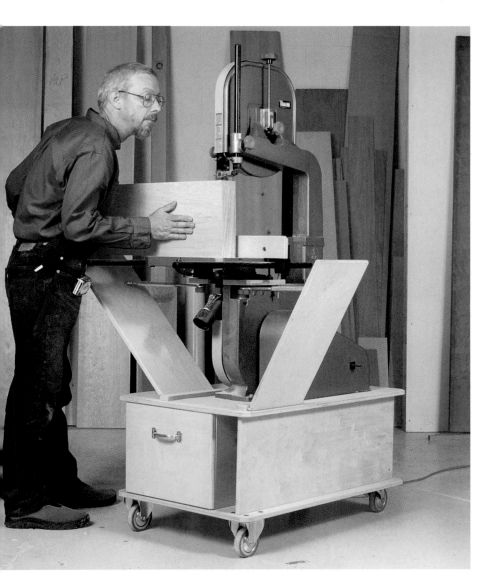

BUILD A BETTER BASE. By replacing the base on a standard 14-in. bandsaw with a plywood cabinet, you can tackle long cuts or heavy resawing without struggle. Infeed and outfeed supports attached to the base and saw table bear heavy loads so you don't have to.

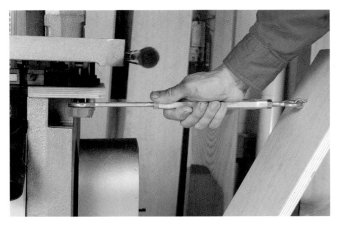

▶ ▲ PLYWOOD BRACES IN PLACE. Adding the infeed and outfeed supports is a snap. One end butts against a stop, and the other hooks to a knob attached to the underside of the saw's table. Adjust the metal rod until the support is level with the tabletop.

▲ FOLD DOWN; FLIP UP. Sidefeed tables help support long crosscuts but can get in the way during rip and joinery cuts. The solution: a hinged table that hangs out of the way. To use it, you simply swing it up and place a T-shaped leg (stored on its side under the outfeed table) underneath.

Choose Your Top Material Wisely

AVAILABLE SHOP SCRAPS USUALLY MAKE GOOD CONSTRUCTION MATERIAL for machine support tables in the shop, especially for the structural bases or framework you might need. But the tops of these tables deserve special treatment. First, a flat top is essential. Second, work should slide easily over its surface. And third, the top must hold up to abuse from heavy timbers or other rough lumber pushed and thrown onto its surface.

Shop-grade plywood is strong and makes a durable base for a top, although medium-density fiberboard (MDF) is flatter and will provide just as much support if properly braced from below. For maximum wear, glue a sheet of countertop-grade plastic laminate over your top material. This stuff is practically indestructible and provides a smooth surface for work to glide over without sticking. A lower-cost alternative is to simply build a top from melamine, which has a smooth yet tough coating that can withstand repeated wear.

◄ MORE THAN JUST OUTFEED. A movable outfeed table means you can use it for other work. Paul Anthony's table stands alone without attaching to the saw, allowing him to access the back of the saw when needed and to use the table elsewhere in the shop for staging assemblies or finishing work.

◄ ▲ GET THE HEIGHT RIGHT. For effective and snag-free outfeed, make sure the table is slightly below your saw's surface. Grooves routed in the top allow clearance for jigs and miter gauges, and an outlet strip screwed to one leg offers easy access for using power tools.

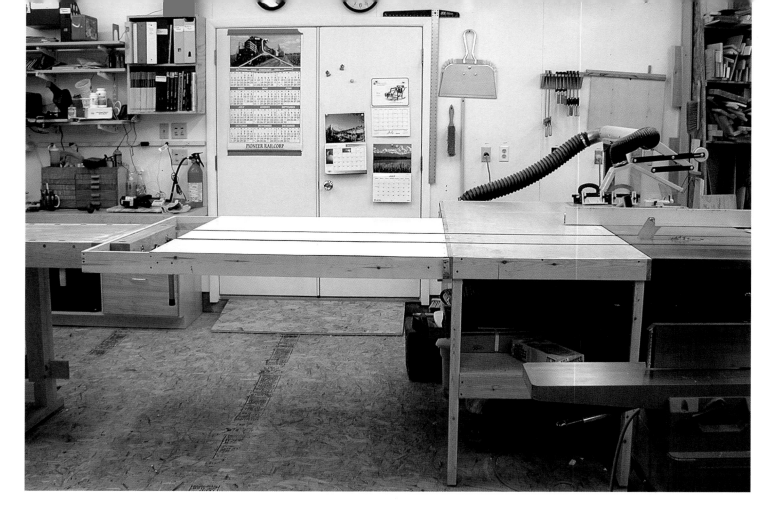

▲ ▶ ▼ EXTRA TABLE IN A JIFFY. A removable, add-on outfeed table increases support capacity and can be stowed when not in use. One end of Spence DePauw's table clamps in a bench vise. The other end fits over a lip in his fixed outfeed table, making installation and removal quick and effective.

▶ ▼ TABLE SAW ENCLOSURE. If you have the space, surrounding your saw with a work surface provides solid outfeed and sidefeed support as well as an extra workstation. The tables in Marc Adams's school shop are built from a framework of 2x8s ripped in half, jointed straight, then screwed together and leveled flat.

▲ THREE SAWS IN ONE. For serious production work, two or more saws combined into one sawing station let you mill wood and cut joints without breaking down your setups. The three cabinet saws at Placeways Woodworking share a central shop-built table, which doubles as an auxiliary work surface.

▲ LOAD ON THIS. Overcome the back-breaking hassle of getting heavy sheets onto the table saw with a tilt-top plywood cart. Fred Sotcher's handler starts in loading mode with its L-shaped top tilted vertically, letting you easily lift a sheet on edge and onto the top.

▲ UNLOCK AND TILT. The top unlocks by releasing a pin, allowing you to easily pivot it horizontally with a full sheet in place. A ³/₄-in.-dia. steel shaft runs through two pillow blocks, affording strong support for the top and smooth pivoting action.

▲ READY FOR CUTTING. Once the top is level, the sheet becomes even with the saw's surface. With the casters in locked position, it's a simple matter of pushing the sheet into the saw.

Auxiliary Tables

THERE ARE MANY TYPES OF TABLES AND WORK SURFACES that will add greater capacity to your shop. One of the biggest hurdles to overcome is making wide crosscuts on the table saw because the stock miter gauge is too skimpy to provide decent support. A crosscutting sled that rides in your saw's miter grooves is one answer. But there are other possibilities, too, such as aftermarket sliding tables.

There are also tables that increase the capacity of other tools, such as the router or the drill press. Drill-press tables aren't particularly well designed for woodworking, and an upgrade here can pay big dividends. Routers are easily converted into router tables by installing oversized baseplates and turning them upside down. A router table can be as simple as a bench-mounted device or can be more involved by incorporating it into your table saw setup or as stand-alone tables.

▲ SAW WIDE STOCK ON A SLED. **Make reliable crosscuts in wide panels with a crosscut sled, a handy item if you build cabinets. Paul Anthony's design slides in the saw's miter grooves via wood runners attached underneath. An adjustable stop makes for accurate repeat cuts.**

▶ CROSSCUT ALL THE TIME. **You can transform a spare table saw into a dedicated crosscut machine by mounting a permanent top that slides on rods and bearings. Randy Schull's aluminum table is made from two pieces to allow for blade clearance and features a stout fence to support long stock for precision crosscuts.**

Stow the Fence

THERE ARE NUMEROUS TIMES you'll want to remove the fence from your tool for making specialty cuts. Bandsaw, router, and drill press fences usually don't pose many problems, as they're typically small enough to stash in an out-of-the-way and safe spot. But table saw and sliding-table table saw fences are longer, heavier, and often need to be put on and off in a moment's notice, making it a hassle if they're stored away from the machine. Here are two ideas for keeping your fences close at hand and ready for action.

◄ RIP FENCE ALWAYS READY. Use the space under your sidefeed table to stash the rip fence. Russ Marie fastened a three-sided plywood box to the underside of his table, sized to fit his fence. When not in use, the fence is out of the way of the operator, but it easily pulls out for reattaching to the saw top.

► LEG BLOCKS MAKE A SHELF. Storing the fence for a sliding table near your saw is convenient. Make use of the space under the table's support structure by bolting plywood blocks to each of the two legs. The fence sits atop the blocks, and small brass washers create a lip to hold the fence in place.

► ENCLOSED SUPPORT. Aftermarket sliding tables can crosscut really big stock, but their open gridwork is a target for nasty finger catches and dropped work. The author capped his grid by first lowering the table through elongated bolt holes, then topping it with $\frac{1}{2}$-in.-thick multiply plywood covered with durable plastic laminate.

◄ DRILLING UPGRADE. **Top your stock drill-press table with a bigger table for better performance and increased support. Paul Anthony's addition sports T-tracks mounted flush with its surface, which allows for easy positioning of an aftermarket fence, hold-downs, and other jigs made for the tracks.**

▼ ANGLES ARE NO PROBLEM. **Drilling angled holes is a cinch if you clamp an angled ramp to the drill press table. Mario Rodriguez slopes his plywood table 10° to make the specific holes he typically drills. Create the angle you need by increasing or decreasing the height of the riser block.**

▲ TABLE SAW TURNED ROUTER. Take advantage of your table saw's sidefeed table by mounting a router underneath. You can use the saw's rip fence, too, by adding wood blocks that let you adjust the bit opening so you can tailor the setup for any routing procedure.

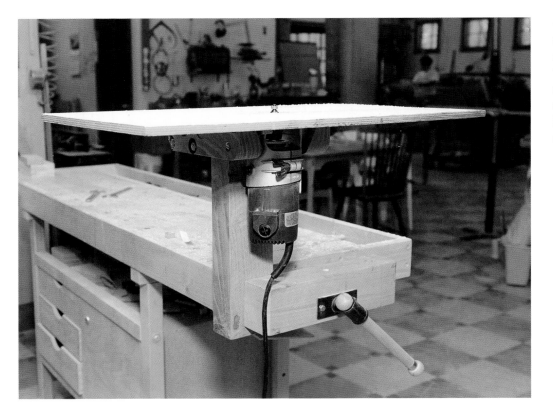

◄ A TABLE THAT DISAPPEARS. Router tables don't need to be fancy or take up precious shop space to work well. This bench-mounted version clamps quickly and securely in a vise and offers a more convenient routing height. Once routing is done, simply unclamp and store it on a shelf.

Mobile Workstations

I T's often essential to move a tool to provide clearance for long or awkward workpieces. And taking the tool to the work is a handy feature if the work is large or unwieldy. Making your tools mobile is the answer. Even large machines, such as table saws and bandsaws, can be equipped with casters or commercial mobile bases that let you push hundreds of pounds of cast iron where you need it.

Stability is a key issue when making a tool portable. Not only must the machine be anchored firmly to its base, but it also should be easy to move without tipping and then sit rock-solid once it's in place. Large-diameter caster wheels roll more smoothly than smaller ones over uneven shop floors. And locking casters that lock the wheel rotation as well as its swiveling action are best. Machines bolted to sturdy, shopmade bases work well, especially if you load them up with weighty accessories to give them extra mass.

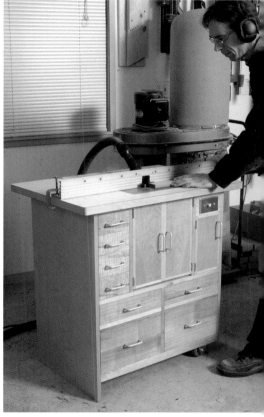

▼ STABLE WHEN DOWN. **A solid panel on one side and casters on the other provide a firm stance once a tool is in position. To move his router table, Paul Anthony simply lifts the non-caster end and wheels the tool where it's needed.**

◄ CHOP WHERE YOU WANT. **A movable chopsaw comes in handy when adding trim or other moldings to large cabinets. Walt Segl's mobile cabinet supports his miter saw at a comfortable working height. Stabilize the assembly by bolting the saw to the cabinet and loading up the inside with heavy gear.**

◀ ▲ DRILLING FROM A CORNER. A mobile benchtop drill press lets you park the tool out of the way, then pull it out for drilling long work or to facilitate cleanup. A bank of drawers stocks bits and accessories, adding necessary weight to keep the center of gravity low.

▶ BENCHTOP MADE BIGGER. A bank of old file drawers supports a benchtop-style press and provides plenty of storage to boot. Russ Marie added a heavy maple top to create a larger workstation and mounted the assembly on a shop-made dolly for easy transport.

Multipurpose Setups

W ORKSTATIONS AND MACHINES THAT PERFORM MULTIPLE TASKS save space and create more efficiency in the shop. Many woodworkers invest in combination machines, which typically center around a table saw that combines a jointer, shaper, and often a mortiser. But you can save money and equip your own machines and workstations to serve several functions.

Some of this work involves careful machine placement, such as stacking two planers together so you can take rough and finish cuts without changing setups or moving stock all over the shop. Or you can build stations that accommodate several machines in one spot, saving you the hassle of moving you and your work from spot to spot and letting you pack it all away at the end of the day to conserve space and keep things tidy.

◄ ROUGH AND FINE STACKED TOGETHER. Placing a high-speed benchtop planer and a lower-speed, heavy-duty machine together lets you take both rough and fine cuts with the same setup. Anatole Burkin mounted his benchtop machine on a sturdy plywood platform that he bolted to the floor-model planer.

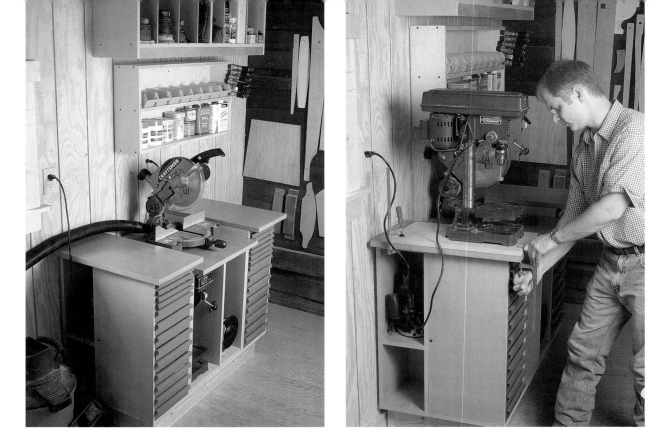

▲ THREE TOOLS IN ONE. **A workstation that accommodates several machines saves space and increases efficiency. Matthew** Teague's chopsaw stand is ideal for mitering and other crosscut work. When needed, the drill press and grinder stowed below are easily clamped to the work surface above and put into action.

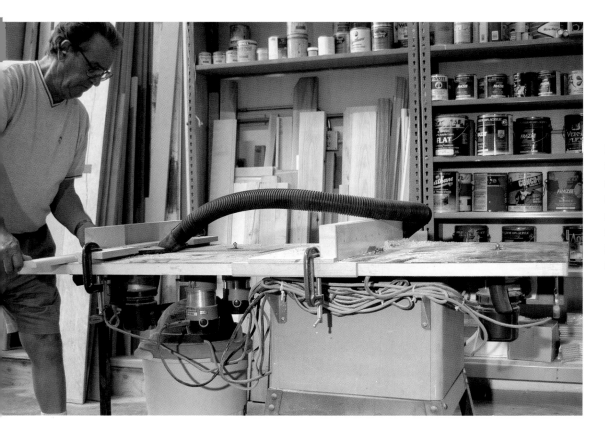

◄ TABLE SAW TURNED MILLING MACHINE. Fitting a router table with multiple routers allows you to keep a variety of router setups in place for more efficient cuts. Arthur Paul mounted an oversized top to an old contractor-saw base, then hung four routers under the top to create his multiple milling machine.

Sharpening Stations

YOU CAN'T BEAT HAVING A DEDICATED SHARPENING SETUP in the shop. With sharpening gear always at the ready, you're much more likely to stop and sharpen your tools instead of ignoring those blunt edges.

The key to a good setup is the height at which you place your gear, such as grinding wheels and honing stones, and having good lighting. In general, it's best to grind high, or roughly level with your elbows, so you maintain a consistent grip as you move the tool over the grinding wheel. Honing should take place down low, or at palm level, so you can place your upper body weight over the tool to support it while providing adequate pressure over your stones. Good light can come from nearby windows or from adjustable light fixtures that allow you to aim light at the precise area you need to see.

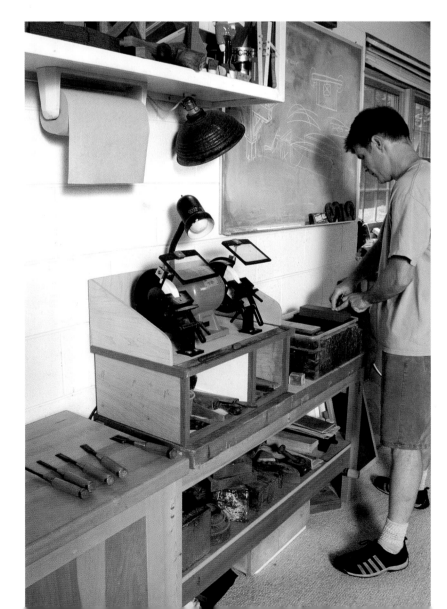

▲ WET AND READY. Keeping waterstones wet is an important aspect of using these tools. Try saturating stones in an inexpensive plastic box filled with water, then hone them with the stones resting on wood ledgers above water. An outer wooden box stiffens the inner box and supports the stones during use.

◄ ONE SPOT FOR BOTH. It's best to set up a grinding wheel and stones in the same area, each at comfortable working heights. The tool rest on the grinding wheel should be about level with your elbows, while waterstones that sit atop a honing box should be at wrist height.

▼ GRANITE ROCKS. A piece of dead-flat granite is great for holding honing stones as well as for truing them when necessary. Tom Dumke installed the granite counter over a shopmade cabinet and tucked the whole affair in a corner of the shop to save space.

▲ OCCASIONAL GRINDER. A grinding wheel isn't typically an everyday tool. It can quickly clutter your workspace but not when you attach it to a pull-out tray. Curtis Erpelding's grinding setup pulls out on metal slides when needed, then rolls back out of the way when sharpening is done.

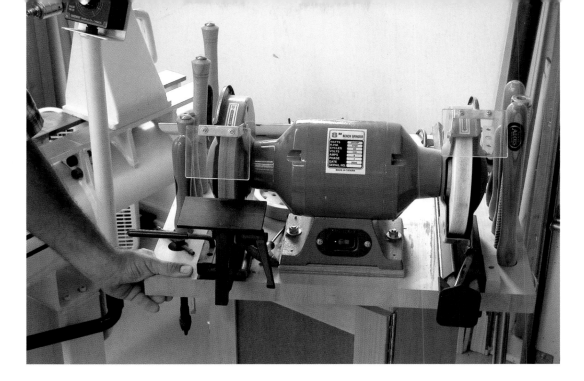

▲ ◄ TURN AND SHARPEN. Woodturning requires supersharp tools that need to be touched-up often. To minimize interruptions, Walt Segl located a grinding station adjacent to his lathe, with holders for his chisels and a swiveling top that lets him sharpen without breaking his stride.

Sanding Centers

OUTFITTING THE SHOP WITH A DECENT SANDING SETUP will make your sanding chores more effective and more bearable. For example, sanding small work can pose a challenge if you can't effectively hold it to prevent oversanding or accidentally rounding over edges. And simply sanding large work on an available work surface can lead to scratches or uneven results. Plus, you'll want to find ways of collecting the fine dust that sanders produce so you can reduce the health hazards.

The good news is that you can set up any number of sanding stations that deal with these problems. A station with built-in dust collection is most convenient, allowing you to smooth small or large work without having to worry about dust. If space is a problem, you can capture dust with a temporary setup without installing a permanent fixture.

▲ CATCH IT AT THE SOURCE. A shop-built dust-extraction panel can catch the clouds of dust that spew from pad sanders and can be placed wherever sanding occurs. Scott Brown made a box from pegboard with a port that connects to his shop's dust-collection system.

◄ PORTABLE BOX. A portable sanding box connected to a dust collector lets you set up a sanding station when you need to, then stash it when you're done. John McDermott's sanding setup has a peg-board top to let air pass through and is covered with rubber carpet underlayment to cushion the work.

► DEDICATED TABLE. Large work is best sanded on a large table, like the one shown here at Placeways Woodworking. The top is covered with carpet underlayment to protect the work. Wood stops at each end secure the underlayment and let you butt small workpieces against them for clamp-free scraping or sanding.

▲ BUILT-IN BOX. A wall-mounted sanding table is a convenient setup for small and large items and won't clutter your bench in the middle of a project. Pegboard makes a sturdy top and promotes airflow. A scrap of carpet on top of the box protects work from scratches.

A BOX THAT REALLY SUCKS

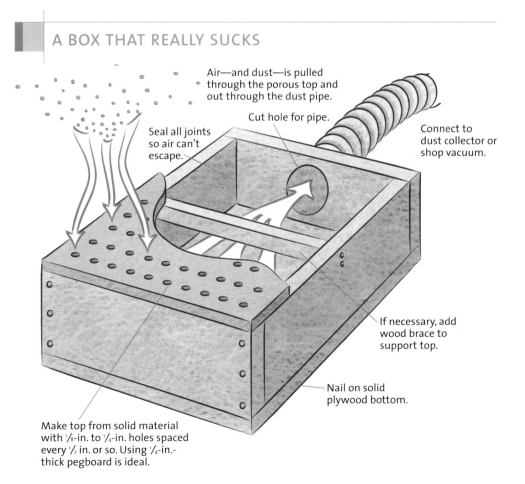

Air—and dust—is pulled through the porous top and out through the dust pipe.

Cut hole for pipe.

Connect to dust collector or shop vacuum.

Seal all joints so air can't escape.

If necessary, add wood brace to support top.

Nail on solid plywood bottom.

Make top from solid material with 1/8-in. to 1/4-in. holes spaced every 1/2 in. or so. Using 1/4-in.-thick pegboard is ideal.

► SAND IT ALL WITHOUT DUST. A dedicated bench fitted with dust collection is the best of both worlds, letting you sand small and large items on a sturdy platform while containing dust. Russ Marie's arrangement features a fan inside the cabinet that pulls dust through the open-framework benchtop and into a filter system.

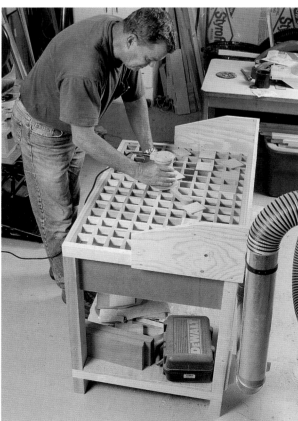

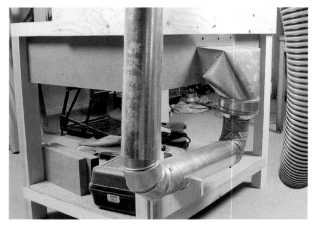

◄ ▲ WOOD STOPS INSTEAD OF CLAMPS. Wood blocks fit into the open gridwork on the top of this sanding table, allowing the user to hold small work without clamps. Peter Brown fitted an enclosed box under the top with a sheet-metal air-conditioning duct, then connected his shop's dust system.

▼ ▶ SAND ON YOUR MAIN BENCH. You can use your bench for general woodworking as well as for sanding if you fit it with slotted panels for dust collection. The panels on Bill Sams's bench sit on wood ledgers above a hollow box, providing plenty of support and easy access in case of clogs.

Vacuum Veneering Setups

ENEERING LARGE-SCALE WORK BY VACUUM is an emerging technology for the small-shop woodworker, thanks in part to affordable vacuum pumps, bags, and other membranes. But using and setting up these systems require some clever engineering so that everything fits within the confines of the shop. Unless you work with veneer full time, you'll benefit from a system that breaks down or stows away easily, so you can go back to "regular" woodworking without cluttering the workspace.

It's important to make sure your veneering setup includes a stable, flat surface on which the work sits, since any curvature will result in unwanted bends in the work itself. Torsion-box construction is a reliable method for building large, flat tables and can be used to advantage when setting up a veneering station. At the very least, use plenty of bracing to withstand the weight of the work as well as the effects of gravity.

▲ VANISHING VENEERING. If veneering is a part-time activity, you'll appreciate a veneering table that moves out of the way. Joe Tracy's table folds down onto a pair of sawhorses for use, then stows against the wall when done. For even more space, the entire wall rolls out of the way with the setup in place.

▲ BUILT LIKE A BRICK. Vacuum veneering requires a sturdy, flat table for successfully flat veneer jobs. Gabe Aucott's rolling table is made from 2x4 stock with a plywood top and is heavily braced to prevent sag. Veneer and vacuum pump storage is built in.

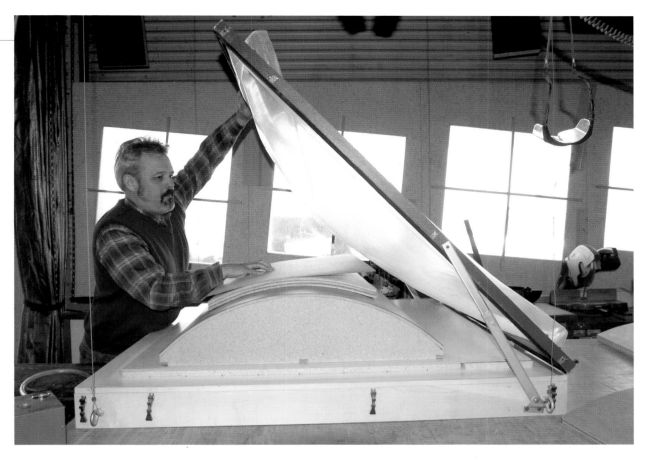

▲ ▼ ► UP AND AWAY. Use an existing flat surface and your shop's ceiling to keep veneering clutter at bay. Miles Clay stows his vacuum-frame system by first removing any bending forms, then hoisting the frame on cables and pulleys directly above his table saw's outfeed table, where it waits for another veneering session.

Finishing Areas

WIPING ON AN OIL FINISH is usually not a big deal and can be done successfully on an available bench—a good reason why many woodworkers choose this finishing system. But brushed and sprayed finishes can pose a challenge to many, with ambient dust settling on top of workpieces and overspray clouding up the air and landing on everything in sight. A decent finishing area is a must if you're going to brush on slow-drying finishes or use a spray gun.

After applying the finish, it has to dry unmolested and free from airborne dust. Even oil finishes need a safe place to dry or rough surfaces result. The trick is to use a suitable drying rack that can store your work in a clean space while the finish cures.

▶ THROW-TOGETHER BOOTH. Blow fumes out of your garage with a cardboard corral and a strategically placed fan. Chris Minick's setup incorporates a furnace filter fitted to a cardboard enclosure, with a fan placed in front of the booth. A router speed control slows the fan to reduce overspray and bounceback.

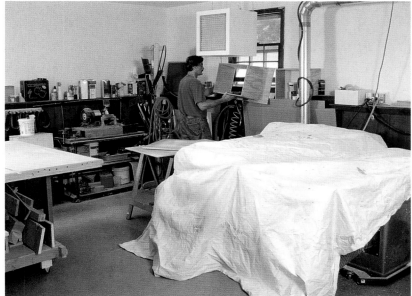

▼ USE WHAT YOU HAVE. **You can spray in the shop with a little creativity. First, cover machine surfaces with dropcloths. Anatole Burkin then installs a plywood duct extension between his shopmade air cleaner and window frame to exhaust overspray and fits the cleaner with a coarse furnace filter.**

▲ RACKS THAT FOLD. **If space is tight, a folding rack can provide some breathing room. The racks in Tom Dumke's finish room are made from 2x4s hinged to the studs in the wall, with removable sticks for supporting different-sized work. When drying is done, the racks fold conveniently onto the wall.**

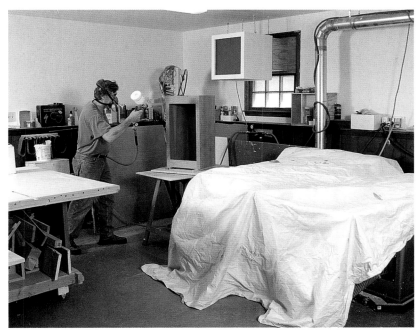

▲ ▶ HANGING SPRAY SETUP. Dangling your work lets you easily spray all sides. Miles Clay uses chains and hooks mounted to a frame with hook eyes in the work in inconspicuous areas for fast hanging. When done, the frame rises on pulleys to the ceiling, freeing up shop space.

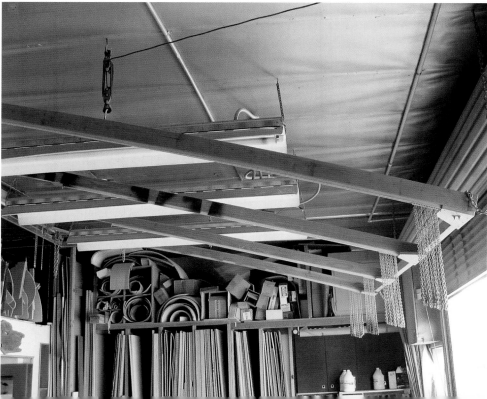

SUPPORTS THAT MOVE. A drying rack that's adjustable lets you alter the layout to support any shape or size work. Gabe Aucott's system relies on French cleats mounted horizontally to the wall. Each support is beveled to match the cleats, allowing you to adjust layout on the fly.

4

Storage Solutions

Having a place for all your gear is one of the keys to a successful—and comfortable—working space. With designated spots for all your supplies, including lumber, tools, hardware, and sanding accessories, you'll know where everything is so you can get to it without spiking your blood pressure. Plus, logical storage solutions prompt you to put stuff away at the end of the day, so everything is ready and waiting the next time. This level of organization makes a shop more efficient and creates a place where great work gets done.

The storage solutions on the following pages come from both big and small shops and embrace many woodworking disciplines, from hobby work and professional cabinetmaking to specialty crafts such as turning, carving, and instrument making. You're sure to find several solutions to fit your own shop's needs. Keep in mind that storing your gear is an evolutionary process, and you're bound to gather more things as you progress—especially tools. Organize with this in mind by incorporating extra space in your current setups for those inevitable future acquisitions.

◀ CLAMPING DISPLAY. **Good use of wall space allows you to see your clamp collection for easy pickings during construction and assembly. Organizing tools in this manner means less hassle rooting around later and proves a blessing for time-sensitive jobs such as glue-ups.**

Stashing Wood

KEEPING TRACK OF YOUR RAW MATERIAL means sorting it by type: solid-wood planks, man-made panels such as plywood, MDF, and other sheet goods, and veneer. Your level of organization should include storing "shorts," those offcuts and other small parts that no one has the willpower to throw away. You'll also want to stash any work in progress so it's in good shape when you come back to work.

Having lumber neatly separated by category allows you to access it with ease and—equally important—to stash new supplies in the right place as they arrive in the shop. Proper storage also ensures that wood remains in good condition, without gathering excess moisture or getting damaged from lying on a dirty, damp floor. Keeping stock flat so it doesn't warp and twist is another key objective.

▼ A WORLD OF WOOD. **Flip through a series of veneered panels like the pages of a book to check color and pattern for yourself or customers. Each removable panel hangs on dowel pins and has a different species on each side. Frank Klausz's collection totals more than 50 woods.**

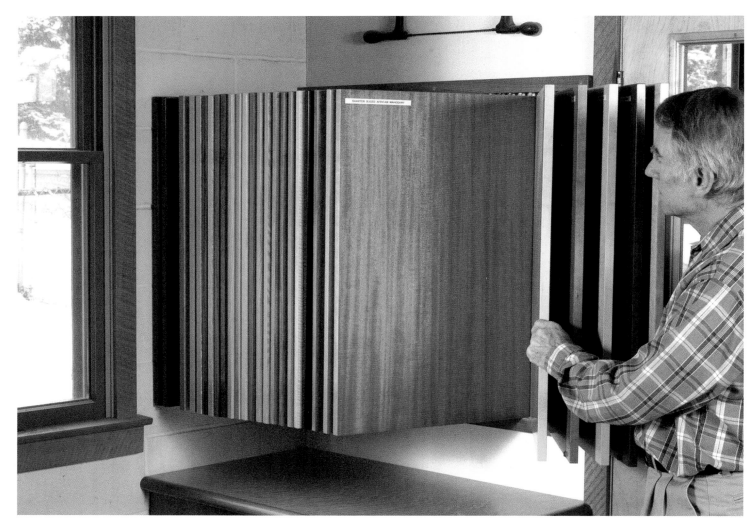

▲ OVERHEAD MAKES SENSE. Don't overlook the space above your head for stashing planks. Rafters make excellent support systems for long and heavy loads such as lumber. But make sure rafters are rated to take the load, and have a ladder handy to access your stock.

▶ OUTSIDE UNDER COVER. An outdoor shed, with lumber stacked flat and aboveground, can store the bulk of material before it's brought into the shop to acclimate to indoor conditions. Good air circulation promotes drying, but open sides should be closed with tarps during heavy weather.

LUMBER STORAGE

▶ STACK AND CUT. Maximize shop space by incorporating a chopsaw station as part of your lumber rack. This sturdy boxed platform sits at a convenient height, allowing you to easily pull boards from the rack and chop them to length.

◀ IN THE BOULE. If you work with whole logs, allocate enough space for storing flitch-cut planks in the order they were sawn. Their sheer bulk helps keep them flat, and stacking in order makes sequential matching for color and grain much easier when selecting parts for projects.

◀ STURDY ADJUSTMENT. A commercial metal rack mounted to the wall will hold hundreds of pounds of stock horizontally. Adjustment is easy with steel arms that can be aligned on their pilasters to the desired shelf height.

▼ ▶ LARGE AND SMALL STUFF. Combining storage for different-sized items means you'll save room. Spence DePauw's rack uses metal pipe that's angled up 10° so heavy boards stay put. Plastic tubes slipped over the pipe prevent staining. The hollow pipe offers a convenient spot for dowels.

◄ ▲ ACCESSIBLE, VERSATILE, AND FLAT. A freestanding rack lets you access stock from all sides. Paul Anthony's rack includes a middle bay for plywood. To keep boards flat, Anthony levels the rack to the floor by raising or lowering lag bolts mounted in the feet.

FREESTANDING LUMBER RACK

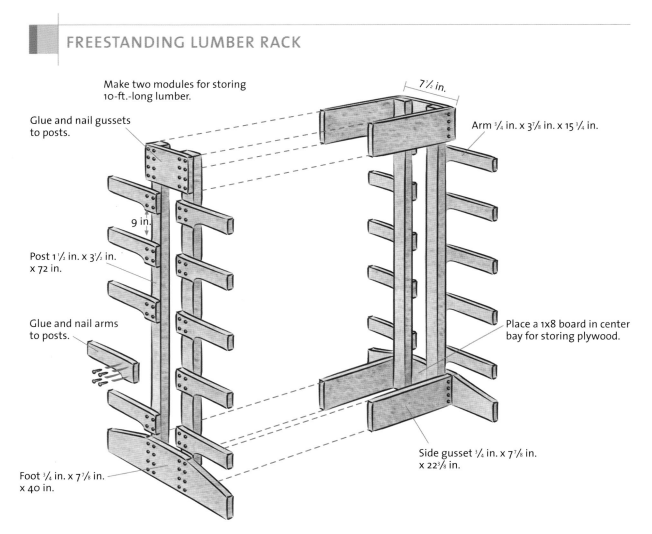

Make two modules for storing 10-ft.-long lumber.

Glue and nail gussets to posts.

7½ in.

Arm ¾ in. x 3⅞ in. x 15¾ in.

9 in.

Post 1½ in. x 3½ in. x 72 in.

Glue and nail arms to posts.

Place a 1x8 board in center bay for storing plywood.

Side gusset ¾ in. x 7⅞ in. x 22⅜ in.

Foot ¾ in. x 7⅞ in. x 40 in.

▼ ▶ BIG AND TALL. **Made from heavy timbers tied into the floor and ceiling, the heavy-duty rack at Placeways Woodworking provides plenty of storage with access on all sides. Posts are spaced 18 in. apart, with crossbeams running through them and pinned to prevent racking.**

▲ SEPARATED BY PLYWOOD. A series of notched plywood spacers slip over horizontal cleats in the bays to segregate types and species. When stock depletes or changes, simply move the spacers as required.

▲ TALL AND LEAN. Extra-tall ceilings offer an opportunity to store long boards vertically. In Lon Schleining's shop, short and tall boards are stored upright and divided into bays for convenient sorting.

▶ BAY WATCH. Make sorting planks a breeze by storing them vertically in individual bays grouped by species. Sam Maloof built a plywood base to keep boards off damp floors and added a clip-on rope to prevent unexpected accidents.

PLYWOOD RACKS

▶ TALL AND DEEP. Storing sheet stock horizontally can maximize space for other materials. Each stall in John West's rack is more than 5 ft. tall by 12 ft. deep and holds extra-big sheets such as oversized panels of fiberboard, while leaving room for lumber above.

◀ SORTED BY DOWELS. Spaced every foot or so, closet-rod dowels take up little space and are great for separating plywood sheets without the hassle of building individual bins. Lon Schleining secured the dowels to a cleat nailed to the wall and built a raised platform to keep edges clean and make loading and unloading a snap.

ROLL 'EM IN AND OUT. With metal rollers mounted in front of your plywood rack, you can ease insertion and removal of large, heavy sheets. Make sure the floor of the rack is high enough so sheets clear the top of the rollers.

◀ EASY PICKINGS. Built from plywood, this vertical rack stores full sheets in individual bays, making selection easier because panels can be grouped by species and encouraging panels to stay flat. A raised subfloor keeps panel edges clean, dry, and safe from damage.

Accessing Heavy Sheets

Pulling full sheets from a rack can be troublesome, as the heavy sheets resist being tugged on when there's very little panel for your hands to grasp. To overcome inertia, shape a small hardwood stick with a belly at one end, then slip it underneath a sheet. Step repeatedly on the stick to coax the panel out far enough until you can comfortably grip the leading edge.

▼ ▶ ROCK 'EM OUT. To access a sheet in a vertical rack, cabinet-maker Klaus Hilgers places a bellied stick under an edge, rocking the stick with his foot to coax the panel out a few inches (below). He then grabs the protruding edge to pull out the entire sheet (right).

STORING VENEER

▶ SORTED AND BUNDLED. Presorting your veneer before storing it can save space and time. In Marc Adams's school workshop, veneer is organized by species and stacked in matched sets on plywood shelves, allowing students to pick exactly what they need for their projects.

▲ ACCESSIBLE UP ON HIGH. Make use of what would otherwise be wasted space by building on the ceiling. An overhead rack keeps veneer sheets flat and easy to see and get to. Holes cut into thin plywood mounted below the rack store a variety of dowels.

Keeping Veneer Flat

BUCKLED OR TWISTED VENEERS require flattening before pressing. Preflattening them and then storing them makes sense, so they're always ready to go. Start by spraying or sponging both sides of a sheet of veneer with water to soften its fibers. Wait a minute, then place the wet sheet on a plywood or MDF panel, with a piece of old newspaper in between. (Use old paper; fresh ink can transfer.) Lay a second piece of newspaper on top, and cover the stack with another MDF panel. Place weights, such as handplanes or bricks, on top, and stash the package on a flat shelf. It will take a week or more to remove the moisture in the veneer, during which time you should replace the damp paper daily. When the paper is dry, leave the package alone until you're ready for pressing.

◀ STACKED LIKE LUMBER. Long veneer bundles can be stored similarly to solid planks. On a metal rack in Frank Pollaro's shop, packages sit on panels of MDF, which keeps them flat. Really buckled veneers have heavy panels placed on top to weight them down and minimize warp.

◄ CHOP AND STORE. The place for off-cuts is where you make them. Paul Anthony's chopsaw station has shelves for small solid-wood leftovers as well as an open cabinet for partial sheets of plywood.

► PURPOSE-BUILT BINS. Keep your offcut bin organized by planning for different sizes. Frank Pollaro's plywood offcut bin has an open bay in front for small pieces. At the back is a deeper bin for taller stock, such as half sheets of plywood or solid-wood rippings.

▲ SIDEFEED SHELVES. Take advantage of what would otherwise be wasted space under machinery. Here, the author screwed cleats onto the shop-built cabinet at right, then bolted similar cleats through the table saw's sheet-metal motor. Plywood placed over the cleats makes instant shelves.

◄ STASH IN THE SIDE. Use the space below your table saw's outfeed table for storing partial panels, so they're ready for cutting when the need arises. Frank Klausz's table is supported by braced sheets of plywood, with a center divider to keep parts organized.

▲ BUCKET BRIGADE. Trash cans and buckets in varying sizes make great instant storage for dowel stock. Long dowels live in taller containers, while shorter offcuts go in short buckets, making small stuff more accessible. A heavy-duty metal trash can stores rod and other metal stock.

▲ LOAD AT THE END. A cabinet under an outfeed table serves double-duty as support for the table and as storage for plywood shorts and solid-wood rippings. Tom Dumke divided the cabinet and installed shelves, neatly compartmentalizing his offcuts.

Recycle Your Wood

IF YOUR SHOP IS CONTINUALLY OVERFLOWING with short stock and storage isn't an option, one place you can put your offcuts is into the hands of others. Chances are there are plenty of area woodworkers, particularly hobbyists, who are eager to make good use of your waste. Place a bin or large container outside the shop, with a sign saying "Free Wood." You'll be pleasantly surprised at the traffic it generates. In no time at all, your shop "scrap" will turn into toys, knickknacks, and other deserving woodwork instead of burdening the local landfill.

▶ DRAWER OF GEMS. Too lovely to throw away, small, precious offcuts fit nicely in shallow or deep drawers, depending on their specific size. Really small pieces live in boxes inside the drawers, keeping treasured wood within reach.

▼ PARTS CART. Work in process needs a safe spot to prevent parts from getting bruised. Curtis Erpelding's aluminum baker's rack, fitted with flakeboard shelves, holds frame pieces and small panels and can be wheeled to where the action is taking place.

Storing Tools

KEEPING TRACK OF TOOLS IS ONLY POSSIBLE when there's a proper place for them. How you store them depends on your collection and what kind of work you do. For example, if you need to carry a small kit of tools, a portable toolbox will fit the bill. On the other hand, if your shop is overflowing with hand tools and small power tools, you'll need various storage schemes, from drawers and shelving to cabinets and wall racks. Don't forget to dedicate a spot (or two!) for all those jigs and other clever devices that accumulate over the years.

The key to storing tools is to group them together by their use. For example, layout and marking tools should live in the same area. Keep power tools together with their accessories, such as routers and their associated edge guides and jigs. With like-minded tools stashed in the same spot, there will be less time spent hunting around for gear during the various phases of building a project.

▲ SIMPLE BUT EFFECTIVE. Open bins and hangers make it easy to access everyday tools. No space is wasted in Sam Maloof's shop, where chairmaking gear is sorted in tins and boxes. The end of a bench makes great storage, too, with nails driven into it so tools can hang right where they're needed.

◄ DRAWERS KEEP YOU ORGANIZED. One of the best ways to store gear is to utilize drawers. Bill Crozier's tool chest sports a series of drawers that allow him to sort tools by category. For example, chisels are placed in adjacent drawers, making it easier to keep track of them.

▲ IN PLAIN VIEW. Shelves made from dimensioned lumber are simple to make and, at about 10 in. wide, are the perfect depth for holding sets of wooden molding planes, joinery planes, and other specialty planes.

▶ HIDDEN BEHIND DOORS. Simple plywood shelves fitted into cabinets underneath a work counter provide plenty of space for utility tools and gear, such as drills, routers, saws, and their toolboxes. Doors reduce clutter and keep out dust.

SHELVES, TRAYS, RACKS, AND CUBBIES

▲ FUNCTIONAL ELEGANCE. Sometimes a tool collection is too beautiful to hide behind closed doors. Simple but refined open shelves showcase a beautiful collection—and make it easy to get to the tools when you need to use them. Walt Segl's set of prized spokeshaves adds a touch of class to his shop.

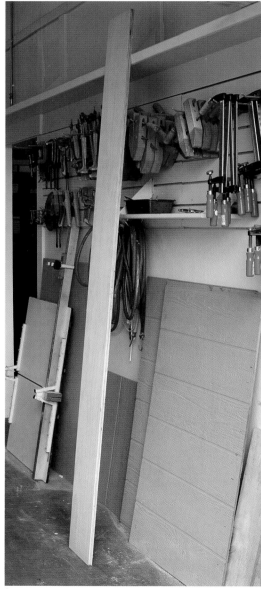

▶ A SAFETY SHELF FOR BOARDS. Rather than propping boards in process against a wall full of gear, rest them against a shelf instead. This keeps wall-mounted stuff free from damage. Arthur Paul mounted his shelf above head height so the edge supports 6-ft. and longer boards while providing storage for small items above.

▲ BOXES BECOME SHELVES. Leftover drawer boxes make modular wall-mounted storage units. Each of the author's boxes can hold its own router with its various accessories, providing easy access and convenient storage.

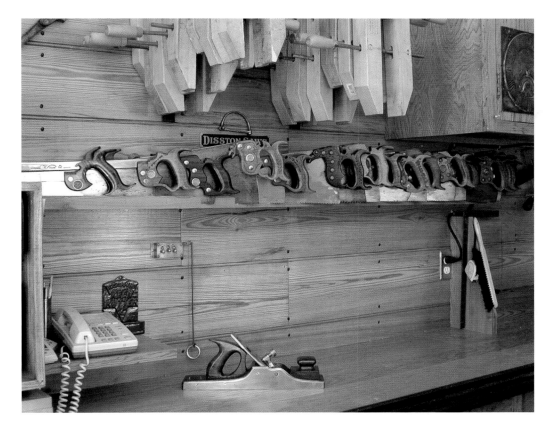

◀ ▲ SAWN SHELF. Innovative saw storage means the saws are ready for use at a moment's notice and don't take up much room. In Jim Moon's shop, a series of angled saw kerfs (above) sawn into the shelf with a thin-kerf circular saw hold a collection of vintage saws upright and in a relatively compact space.

▲ A TRAY OF PLANES. **Planes for everyday use can be stored in an open tray for easy access. The tray in Chris Becksvoort's shop is angled 60°, and planes rest against ledger strips so they stay secure. The top tray lifts up to reveal storage for seldom-used items, such as spare parts, blades, and fences.**

Don't Forget the Accessories

WHEN DECIDING ON A SPACE FOR A PARTICULAR TOOL **or grouping of tools, it's wise to build in a little extra space for all those related items that go with them. For example, when storing handplanes, factor in room for extra blades, spare knobs and handles, and specialty fences. Power tools are just as accessory-hungry as hand tools. Routers, drills, and saws all need similar breathing room for gear such as wrenches, chuck keys, collets, handles, and fences. Keeping accessories with the tools that use them will cut down on time spent searching for the right part when it's needed most.**

▲ SWING OVER THE LATHE. This lathe-tool rack rotates over the ways on a wall-mounted piano hinge, allowing turner Tom Dumke to reach tools without straying from his work. When turning is done, the rack pivots back against the wall and out of the way (right).

▶ GRAB A DRILL. You'll never have to search for the right drill if you store them all within easy sight and access on a wall-mounted rack. The lower shelf of Paul Anthony's rack is drilled to accept the chucks of various drills and angles outward about 20° so handles are easy to grab. A lipped shelf above stores chargers, odd-shaped drills, and accessories.

◄ SANDBOX UNDER CONTROL. **Individual** racks are the perfect size for palm and orbital sanders. The boxes in Palomar College's shop are mounted to wooden disks, with space behind so cords can be wrapped neatly out of the way. This setup works well in a classroom situation or wherever shop tools are shared.

▲ DIVIDED BY SIZE. **Dividers create cubbies** and are spaced to the width of individual planes, saving space while devoting specific spots so tools won't get lost. The heel of each plane rests on a small strip of hardwood, raising the back of the plane to prevent the sharp iron from digging into the shelf.

► SCRAPERS AND MORE. **Smart storage** for hand scrapers and their accessories means providing quick access without taking up space. A rack with angled slots cut in the sides accepts almost any type of scraper, with room for more as your collection grows. Walt Segl added some holes at the top of his rack to store burnishers, too.

CHISEL RACKS

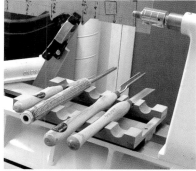

◄ ▲ LOAD AND GO. This simple pine rack can be loaded up with chisels and then brought to the bench for hand-work (left). A rack for lathe tools finds a sturdy spot between the bed's ways thanks to blocks screwed underneath (above).

► PLUGGED PIPES. Make good use of inexpensive PVC pipe to store lathe tools and make them portable as well. Doug Stowe's pipes are mounted to a French-cleat system on the wall and can be moved to the lathe when needed. The top of the pipes are cut at an angle to facilitate loading, and the bottoms are plugged with wood.

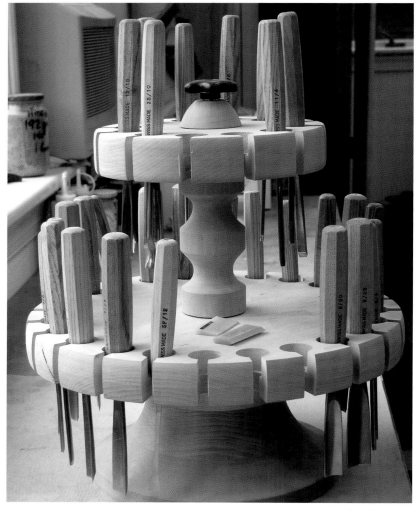

◄ SHARP EDGES IN STYLE. **If you want to move a rack around in the shop, you need to build it so it's easy to slide. Sled-style feet give a freestanding rack a sturdy stance and make it easy to slide the rack along the bench to where the action is.**

▼ CARVING CAROUSEL. **A rotating rack lets you grab the right tool when you need it and is handy for carving, where multiple chisels are necessary. All the parts of Walt Segl's rack were turned on the lathe. The tiers rotate around a central spindle cut into three sections, while a through bolt capped with a lock knob holds the assembly together.**

▲ NO-GLUE DOVETAILS. **Plan for future changes in your tool collection by creating a tool rack that can easily be removed and rearranged. Here, the ends of the author's chisel rack are dovetailed and slide into mating dry sockets cut into the door of a tool cabinet, providing plenty of strength while allowing for reorganization.**

TOOLS ON THE GO

▲ PACKED FOR USE. A handsome toolbox not only lets you carry your tools with you but also lets you set them up in style. Yeung Chan's walnut box is a wonder of organization. Two thin plywood braces pack into the box for transport and then come out to support it at a convenient angle, allowing easy access while working.

▶ TOTING A CLASSIC. The classic tool tote gets an update with a no-slip handle, preventing tools from spilling accidentally. Jan Derr drilled a series of holes in oversized stock and then sawed halfway through the holes to create the handle. Half-blind dovetails and plugged screws join the box sides and center divider.

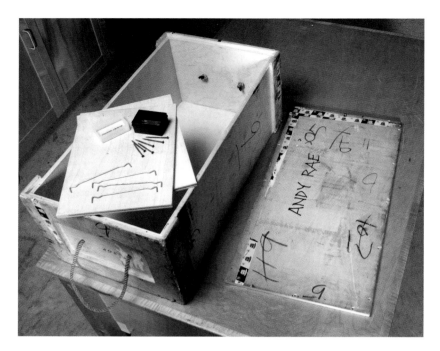

▲ ▶ SHIPPED FOR SETUP. A shipping crate that also functions as display means you don't have to ship shelves, too. Made from strong, multilayered plywood, the author's crate travels with the lid slid under cleats and securely screwed in place. At its destination, the two shelves stowed in the box come out and slide over bent wires fit into holes drilled in the box sides.

Pack Smart

I F YOU'RE TRANSPORTING TOOLS, or shipping them by air or land, it pays to pack them so they arrive safely without damage. Vibration is the number-one tool killer. Tools thrown carelessly into a container will bump into each other until something gives, which usually results in bent parts, split wood handles, or even worse, cracked castings. There are two things you can do to avoid shipping disaster. First, pack tightly. A container without extra space won't leave room for tools to move and jostle about. The second precaution is to wrap tools in cushioning materials. Old T-shirts or finishing rags work well, as does bubble wrap, which contains air bubbles that absorb blows. You can even buy plane "socks" that work well to protect handplanes from bumps as well as inhibit corrosion and rust, which has a habit of finding its way into your carefully packed package.

▲ NO SOCK-IT SURPRISES. Wrapping tools and packing them tightly in a shipping box will prevent nasty surprises. For stowing handplanes, you can buy plane "socks," which cushion blows and are impregnated with silicone to resist moisture and prevent corrosion.

BUILT-IN TOOL CABINETS

▲ PLASTIC AND WOOD. Store-bought utility cabinets come with adjustable shelves and in a variety of configurations. Tall cabinets hold a ton of gear, while base cabinets make great supports under wood counters. Wall cabinets mounted above keep counter clutter to a minimum.

◄ ▲ ► LOADED AND WILLING. A box-style door can hold a ton of tools if you account for the added weight. Strong hinges and floor support do the trick on this plywood, wall-mounted tool cabinet at Palomar College. Instructor Chris Feddersohn opens the door smoothly, thanks to a fixed castor bolted under the door (left).

▲ ◄ AN UN-PLAIN CABINET. Storage cabinets don't have to look utilitarian. Jim Moon built this cabinet from cherry with panels of Brazilian rosewood. Inside, planes sit on their sides in shallow cutouts in the shelves, with a center drawer for extra cutters.

◄ THIN IS IN. At about 10 in. deep, this narrow base cabinet is perfect for holding power tools without taking up precious shop space. An added benefit is that its shallow depth prevents you from cramming tools into the back, where they quickly become inaccessible.

▼ CORNER CACHE. Don't forget to use valuable corner space for storage. Corner cabinets like this curly cherry one in Jim Moon's shop can house tools in drawers and on a shelf, with drills, braces, and saws mounted to the cabinet's angled sides.

▲ ▶ SPACE SAVER. **Just because you don't have a lot of wall space doesn't mean you can't store a lot of tools. A cabinet with a trifold door looks slim on the wall but opens to reveal its cavernous capacity. Fully open, Pat Edwards's case is almost 6 ft. wide and stores multiple sets of carving chisels on shallow racks.**

▶ BLADES AND OTHER BITS OF GEAR.
Storing blades safely and so they're
easily accessible is a challenge. A
blade box with grooves cut in its top,
bottom, and back holds the blades
securely and safely so that you can
easily see what you need.

▲ BITS ONLY. A shallow wall cabinet is
best for storing individual bits, taking
up little space while keeping cutters
accessible. Tom Dumke's router bits sit
in holes drilled in angled shelves, providing plenty of clearance for easy
insertion and removal.

▶ YOU DON'T ALWAYS NEED A WALL.
Small cabinets can be mounted on a
column directly above the tool that
uses them. This router bit storage cabinet packs bits as well as boxed sets,
all housed in a conventional wall cabinet located above the router table.

TOOL DRAWERS

► SORT ON THIS. A pop-out tray offers a convenient spot for organizing gear as it's pulled from drawers. A spring-activated touch-latch in the author's tool cabinet allows the tray to extend with the push of a finger. The leather-topped tray helps cushion tools and delicate edges.

▼ PROTECTED FROM KNOCKS AND MOISTURE. Felt-lined drawers cushion chisels and other edge tools to prevent them from banging into each other. Throw a few packets of desiccant into the drawer to keep steel from rusting.

▶ ▲ INDIVIDUAL FIT. French-fitted drawers, which have recesses cut out for individual tools, keep items such as wrenches in specific spots, making them easier to find if they're missing (above). A pull-out drawer inside a cabinet uses the same European technique to store rasps and files (left).

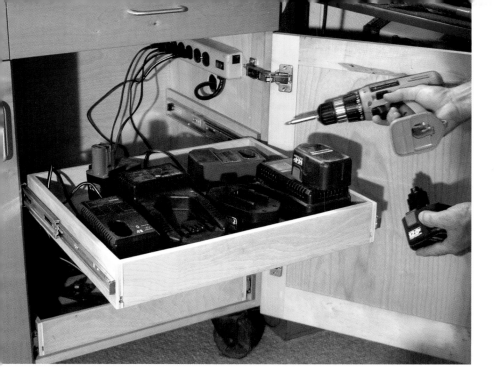

◄ POWER DRAWER. Battery chargers for cordless drills need to be plugged in, taking up valuable space and outlets. But not if you have a pull-out drawer inside a cabinet. Chargers are connected to a power strip mounted inside the cabinet to keep everything out of sight until it's time to recharge.

▼ THIN AND CURVY. Thin drawers take up little room and are perfect for storing slender tools such as chisels. As a design detail, the front of the drawer is curved so it resembles molding and blends in with its opening when shut.

▲ ▶ FILING TOOLS. Old metal filing cabinets can be put to use again as a safe haven for routers and sawblades. The heavy-duty slides in Russ Marie's recycled cabinets can carry the hefty weight. A slotted board in the bottom of a drawer keeps blades separated to preserve fragile carbide teeth.

ORGANIZING BITS AND BLADES

◀ ▲ BIT SHELVES. Metal racks with adjustable shelving store bits and accessories in plain view. Drill bits live in index cases or in holes drilled in blocks of wood. Router bits sit upright in fiberboard panels that have holes drilled in them for commercial plastic bit sleeves.

▶ BIT TRAYS. Pull-out bit drawers are simple to make and store cutters where they're needed most. Drill the tray for the diameter of your bit shanks, then glue on a front equal to the height of your tallest bit.

▲ ▶ IN-AND-OUTSIDE CABINET. A cabinet that fits all the blades and accessories for one tool is ideal. It's even better if it's portable so it rolls where you need it. Walt Segl's cabinet has a pull-out drawer that holds blades in kerfed blocks. When the hinged lid is lifted, a deep well for storing a tenoning jig and throat plates is revealed.

◄ STACKED SO THE TEETH DON'T TOUCH. A dado blade box that separates individual chippers from the outer scoring blades keeps expensive carbide in top condition. Outer blades rest on recessed blocks glued into the corners of the box, with a cardboard spacer in between.

▲ BOXED FOR SAFETY. Dado blades need careful storage or teeth will get damaged. Lon Schleining's dado box separates individual plates in cardboard sleeves that slip into a custom-sized box. Spacers and stiffeners hang outside the box on a bolt so they don't get lost.

▶ BLADE TRAYS IN A BOX. A small box will fit neatly under the saw, keeping sawblades safe without taking up much space. Pegboard trays hold individual blades and slide in grooves in the sides of Paul Anthony's blade box. Packets of desiccant tossed in the bottom absorb any moisture flowing through the holes in the trays, reducing corrosion.

WALL AND OVERHEAD STORAGE

◀ GRIP AND GO. Screwed to the wall, this magnetized strip will grip any iron gear, such as steel hammers, screwdrivers, wrenches, and chisels. Mount it above the workbench or behind a machine such as a lathe, and tools are always within immediate grasp.

▼ HOOKS STAY SECURE. A standard pegboard fitted with hooks works well for holding tools on a wall. To overcome the tendency for hooks to pull out when tools are removed, these special base pieces and clips install over the hooks and lock them in place. Repositioning hooks is a snap, too.

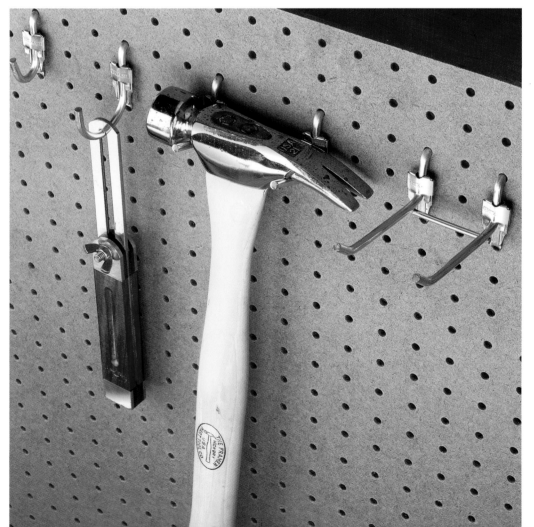

◀ ▼ CUSTOM WALL PANELS. Instead of peg-board, Arthur Paul made his own wall system by milling a series of boards with a T-shaped router bit normally used for cutting slots. Leaving a space between the boards allows him to use standard pegboard hooks for storing tools and jigs on the wall.

▲ ▼ WALLS THAT CAN CHANGE. Pine panels hang on French cleats over a cinder-block wall in Carl Swensson's shop, making it easier to drive nails or screw on wood blocks for holding tools. With no fasteners to undo, the panels are simple to move or modify when a tool collection grows.

REMOVABLE TOOL PANEL

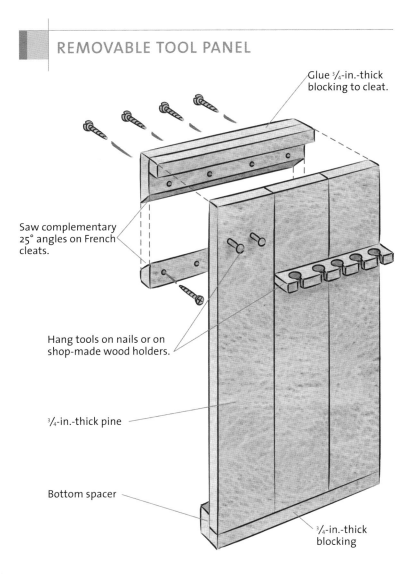

Glue ¾-in.-thick blocking to cleat.

Saw complementary 25° angles on French cleats.

Hang tools on nails or on shop-made wood holders.

¾-in.-thick pine

Bottom spacer

¾-in.-thick blocking

▲ WALL OF JIGS. Plywood strips screwed at two different heights on a wall afford a convenient and sturdy spot for driving screws or nails for hanging jigs. The strip at the top of the wall holds long jigs, while shorter jigs hang on a strip attached at chest height, keeping everything accessible.

◄ HANGING PATTERNS. Use ceilings if you don't have wall space for hanging. Chairmaking jigs in Sam Maloof's shop hang from nails hammered into rafters above, clearing space below while keeping patterns accessible and visible.

MOBILIZING HAND TOOLS

▶ TOOLS ON THE GO. This commercial rolling cart is great for moving hand tools around the shop and comes with large-diameter wheels that negotiate rough floors. The top well is lined with a shopmade wood panel to cushion tools with delicate edges such as chisels and planes.

▼ ROLLING FOR ASSEMBLY. Build a base cabinet, top it with butcher block, and mount it on wheels for a portable bench and toolbox. The author's rolling cabinet houses pneumatic gear such as staple and brad guns, plus other air-driven tools and accessories, with power outlets on each end.

▲ ◄ MOVE IT ALL AT ONCE. A large tool cabinet that's really two parts makes it easier to ship it or move it between locations. For simply moving around the shop, it can be pushed fully loaded on heavy-duty casters, as long as the way is hard and smooth.

Clamping Gear

WOODSHOPS NEVER SEEM TO HAVE ENOUGH CLAMPS, but even the smallest collection needs organizing to make glue-ups go more smoothly. Because of their sheer weight, clamps require careful consideration when being stored in the shop. Hanging them on a spare wall is often the easiest and sturdiest answer, and it makes them readily accessible. Thanks to manufacturers and clever woodworkers, there are many systems for hanging the various kinds of clamps that woodworking requires.

Freestanding clamp racks are another solution. They can be built from standard dimensioned lumber or from found and scavenged materials. Just be sure they're big enough to accommodate future acquisitions, as clamp collections never cease to grow. If portability is important, add wheels under your racks so you can move them to where the clamping action takes place.

▶ CLAMPS TO GO. Try using a metal garbage can for stowing your assortment of shop clamps. Mounted to a plywood base with wheels underneath, you can roll the can to the assembly area and then stash it in a corner when not needed.

◄ ▼ HUNG IN ORDER. Tight organization—keeping like with like—means you can store lots of clamps in a relatively small space. Bar clamps hang from above on wood brackets, while smaller clamps dangle on nails and dowels driven into a panel screwed to the wall. Heavy quick clamps loop over a solid steel rod supported by massive steel brackets bolted to the wall.

◄ CLIPS THAT GROW WITH YOU.
Woodworking catalogs sell all kinds of clamp-hanging gear, such as this bar-clamp system that screws to the wall. You can add or subtract the holder clips, and position them to accommodate thin or wide clamps, adding versatility should your clamp collection grow.

► PEGGED WHERE YOU WANT IT.
Pegboard is easy to mount on the wall, and the clips can be placed where you need them, making this system great for small clamps, such as web clamps, C-clamps, and light-duty bar clamps.

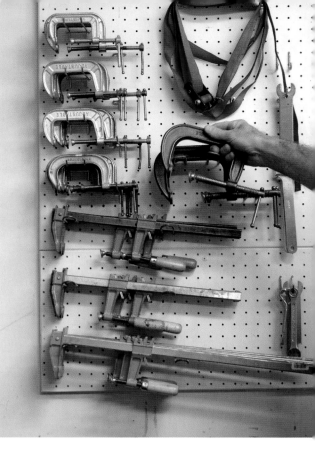

Gripping Walls with Confidence

HANGING TOOLS AND JIGS ON WALLS IS A SENSIBLE WAY to make use of available shop space. But the sheer weight of tools calls for a solid connection to the wall. If the wall is a conventional wood-framed structure, be sure to drive screws through the wall surface and into the studs behind. Avoid drywall fasteners, such as molly bolts, because they don't have the necessary sheer strength for holding the weight of most shop gear.

When attaching to cinder-block or masonry walls, there are many systems and fasteners to choose from. One of the easiest and strongest types is a self-tapping screw sold under various trade names. The beauty of this system is that there's no mounting and remounting of the work on the wall to locate and install the fasteners, as most other systems require. With self-tapping screws, it's an easy, one-shot affair. The screws come in a box in convenient Phillips-style or hex head, with the appropriate-sized carbide-tipped masonry bit. Drill pilot holes through the work you want to attach, hold the work in position on the wall, and drill through the holes and into the masonry with the bit. Then, without moving the work, drive the screws with a Phillips- or hex-head driver bit into the work and the wall for a simplified and worry-free connection.

▲ EASY HANGING. These self-tapping masonry screws save a lot of headaches when it comes to attaching stuff to cinder-block, concrete, or stone walls. You drill through the workpiece and into the wall with the supplied masonry bit, and then, without moving the work, you simply drive the screw home.

▶ BRACKETS FOR BARS. Long clamps with protruding heads, such as pipe clamps or Bessey K Body® bar-style clamps, are a cinch to hang between wooden brackets because you can space the brackets as needed. The author built brackets using lumber-core plywood for strength, then screwed them soundly to the wall.

WALL CLAMP HOLDERS

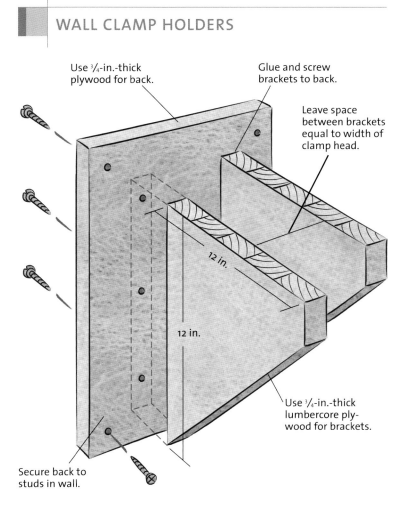

Use ³⁄₄-in.-thick plywood for back.

Glue and screw brackets to back.

Leave space between brackets equal to width of clamp head.

12 in.

12 in.

Use ³⁄₄-in.-thick lumbercore plywood for brackets.

Secure back to studs in wall.

▶ ROLL INTO ACTION. A rolling rack delivers its goods anywhere the clamping action is. A shopmade cart can be as big (or small) as your clamp collection, with sturdy casters to move it alongside machines, workbenches, or assembly tables.

◀ ANGLED RACK. A clamp rack angled back about 10° is enough to keep clamps firmly on crossbars, thanks to gravity. Made from dimensional lumber, the rack is quick to build and offers spots for large and small clamps in a variety of configurations. Be sure to secure the rack to the wall to avoid tip-over.

Hardware and Supplies

FURNITURE HARDWARE COMES IN SUCH A DIZZYING ARRAY OF SHAPES AND SIZES, from nails, screws, and other fasteners to shelf, drawer, door, and specialty cabinet hardware, that storing this eclectic mix in a viable manner can quickly overwhelm an unseasoned woodworker. And don't forget all the other miscellaneous stuff woodworkers collect, such as rolls of tape, wrapping materials, spare parts, electrical goods, and other general shop supplies. Luckily, it doesn't take a degree in engineering to figure out how to sort all this stuff out. With some shelving, a few bins, and drawers with compartments to segregate items, plus the time to sort it all out, everything can be stowed in its proper spot. The best part? Once all the shop's hardware is organized, it's always available when needed and tucked away neatly when it isn't.

▼ PULL OUT TO SEE. **Drawers make excellent storage for small parts. These commercial metal trays are easy to fit into slots cut into the sides of cabinets, letting you build a bank of drawers to store all kinds of hardware and even tools.**

◄ USE ALL YOUR SPACE. **Nails and screws driven into treads and risers under the shop stairs hold an entire collection of tape as well as other supplies. Space is tight, so reserve storage for small items only.**

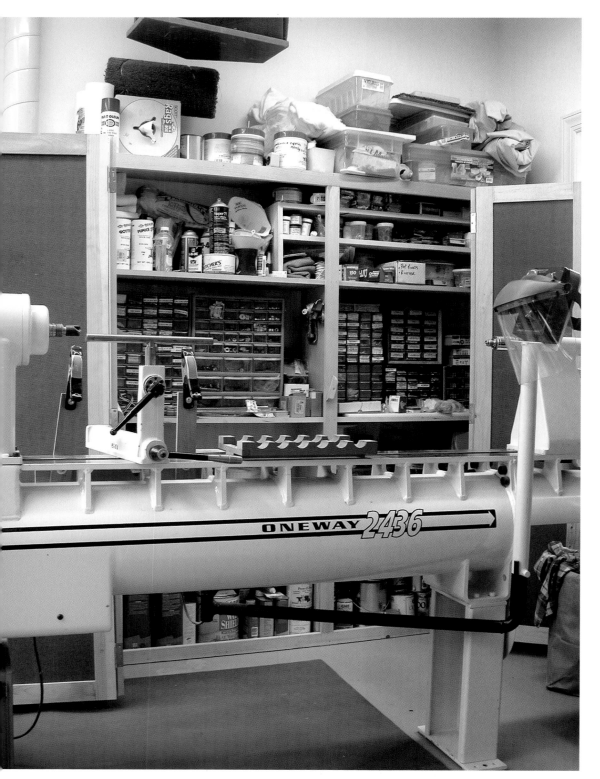

◄ ▲ KEEP OUT DUST. A large cabinet can hold all your hardware and even some other supplies in one place, so you'll never have to remember where to look for things. On his cabinet, Walt Segl used bifold doors, which seal out flying chips and dust when they're closed yet preserve valuable shop space when open.

BINS, SHELVES, AND DRAWERS

▶ SCREWS, STAPLES, AND NAILS. Small plastic bins in a low assembly bench can store screws by size and be fitted with labels so it's easy to find the right size. Pull-out drawers below work well for boxed storage of staples, nails, and other pneumatic fasteners.

▼ FROM SMALL TO BIG. Shelves that taper from narrow to wide mean you can store all sizes of hardware on one shelf. Fitted with small jars at the top, drawer cases in the middle, and large bins below, there are plenty of storage options to accommodate assorted gear.

▲ SMALL STUFF IN SMALL DRAWERS. Commercial drawer bins fit easily on shelves and hold a ton of small gear, from specialty screws and nails to knobs, table hardware, and assorted furniture hardware. The clear drawers let you see what you have and when supplies are low.

◀ HARDWARE BANK. Salvaged index-card cabinets and architectural map drawers are perfect for storing furniture paraphernalia. In Randy Schull's shop, small hardware goes in smaller drawers, while longer gear such as drawer slides and table hardware—as well shop drawings and patterns—fit into the shallow, wide map drawers.

▲ NO-TOOL RELEASE. You can buy metal bins that mount and dismount without tools, letting you take them straight to the job at hand. Once the locking hardware is screwed to the wall, you push a button to unclip the bin from its mount.

▶ LIFT AND GO. Small plastic bins hang one above the other on a metal rack. By simply lifting the bin from its metal frame to remove it, you can sort through contents without straining to see inside.

▲ FITTED HARDWARE. Narrow wood shelves make great spaces for shallow bins and drawer cases. Be sure to buy the containers before constructing the shelves, then build the shelf depth and height to suit.

PORTABLE HARDWARE

▲ TOTING IN TIERS. A compact size doesn't mean small capacity. Made from $1/2$-in.-thick plywood to keep it lightweight and with a stout hardwood handle, the author's hardware tote is really three boxes in one.

▶ STACKED WITH GEAR. Graduated trays lift out to reveal three separate containers. Each box is grooved on the inside to accept $1/8$-in.-thick plastic dividers, keeping hardware and fasteners organized. If future hardware acquisitions call for more space, just increase the size of a compartment by removing a divider.

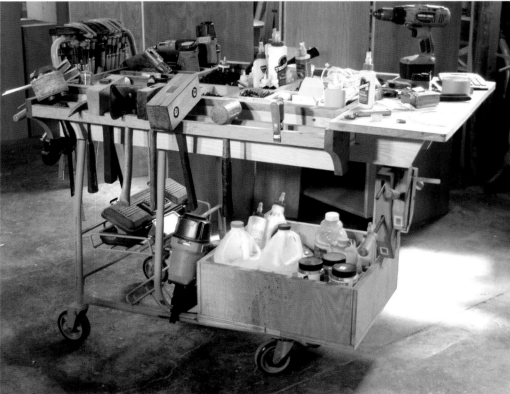

▲ ◄ SHOPPING IN THE SHOP. A converted shopping cart makes a convenient rolling hardware station. For his cart, dubbed the "piercing pagoda," Gabe Aucott added a plywood top fitted with divided boxes to keep screws and other hardware neatly sorted and a staging platform at one end. Below, a large plywood box holds glue and other assembly tools.

Sanding and Finishing Supplies

KEEPING TRACK OF SANDING SUPPLIES, from sheets of sandpaper and sanding belts to sanding tools such as blocks, pads, and related gear, is worth the effort. With abrasives readily available and organized by type, the tiresome chore of sanding will become a wee bit more bearable. Plus, storing abrasives in an orderly fashion means you'll always be using the proper grit, ensuring scratch-free surfaces that are ready for a fine finish.

When it comes to finishing, special care is needed to store finishes safely, especially flammable materials such as certain types of stains, clear coatings like oils, solvent-based lacquers, and polyurethanes, as well as the solvents that go with them. Keeping your finishes on an open shelf not only invites a fire but also degrades the material due to exposure to air and light. The following solutions will keep abrasives and finishes in good shape so that all-important final finish will be flawless.

▼ OVER THE CAN. Discarded coffee cans are a great way to store sanding belts because they help prevent kinks in the belts by keeping the belts rounded. Each can is screwed to a backboard, which in turn is bolted to the wall at a convenient height above the belt sander.

▶ SMALL-SHOP SELECTION. A small cabinet with adjustable shelves lets you sort out sandpaper sleeves and individual sheets of sandpaper, as well as assorted sanding gear, keeping everything readily available. The author's cabinet is made from ½-in.-thick melamine with ¼-in.-thick shelves, with one side divided to hold full-sized sheets.

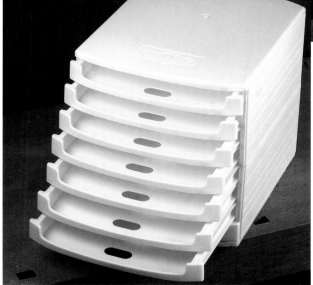

◀ BOXED GRIT. Sized specifically for holding 9-in. x 11-in. sheets of sandpaper or even full sleeves, this commercial sandpaper bin keeps paper organized by size and grit. Each tray can store up to 50 sheets, so you won't run out of abrasive.

▲ STORE IT WHERE YOU NEED IT. Stocking up in the finish room makes sense. A metal cabinet holds flammable finishes, while finish supplies such as filters, rags, and mild solvents sit on a shelf. The work counter below is convenient when preparing finishes.

◄ SAFE AND LONG-LASTING FINISHES. A flameproof metal cabinet is the best bet for storing highly flammable finishes and for keeping the contents in the dark so finishes don't degrade from exposure. Look for doors that lock or have a hasp that accepts a padlock to keep out curious children.

5

Benches and Worktables

Unless you enjoy sitting on the floor to work, you need a decent work surface to complete your shop. A simple bench, with a plywood top screwed to a stout 2x4 frame—perhaps with a vise—can suffice. However, surrounding yourself with multiple work surfaces that offer clever ways of holding your work can make a workshop more versatile and increase your efficiency.

A decent bench should provide a massive and stable work surface for all the pounding and pushing that woodworking demands, a good way of holding stock, and be at the right height so you can work in relative comfort with maximum control. Even with the perfect bench, you'll still run into special circumstances that require alternative approaches, such as raising or lowering the height of your bench for certain tasks, holding odd-shaped work, or even working outdoors or away from the shop. Luckily, there are unique benches that can handle these situations with aplomb.

It's wise to note that a good bench setup includes more than just the bench itself. Your bench should be situated in an open area near tools and supplies so they're easy to get to. Counters with cabinets underneath serve this purpose and are often decent benches in their own right. And when it comes time to assemble your furniture, a well-designed assembly table can make the process go more smoothly.

◄ MORE THAN A BENCH. It's smart to have plenty of workspace surrounding you and your bench. Jim Moon's set-up includes tool storage and a sturdy work counter behind his main bench, tall ceilings, and plenty of floor space to move about.

Workbenches

A T THE HEART OF MANY SHOPS IS THE WORKBENCH. It's where some of the most demanding and time-consuming work gets done. A good bench offers a decent method for holding work, as well as a solid surface for supporting not only your work but also the force you'll use to construct and assemble furniture.

Just as important as your bench is the area where you set it up. Like a well-designed kitchen, the work area around your bench should include an open area that provides a safety margin for moving large pieces about, easy access to tools and supplies, as well as supporting work surfaces, such as countertops and other flat areas where work in progress can be parked. If you routinely tackle unusual stuff, such as holding complex assemblies like chairs, working on extra-tall pieces, or any of the countless odd jobs that woodworkers undertake, look for a specialty bench that's specific to the task.

▲ KEEP TOOLS NEARBY. Benchwork flows more smoothly when hand tools and auxiliary work surfaces are mere steps away. The author's bench area works much like the work triangle in a kitchen, with counters and tool cabinets within reach of his European-style bench.

◄ LOW BENCH ON TOP. Increase your precision and control with tools such as routers by raising your work height—without building a new bench. Tom LeRoy's support bench clamps to his main bench and is braced to provide a rigid work surface.

▲ ▶ OPEN IN THE MIDDLE. A wide bench has the benefit of supporting big pieces, but clamping can be a problem. The solution is a removable center tray, as seen in Pat Edwards' bench, where there's plenty of room to use conventional clamps.

Build a Bench at School

IF YOU'VE EVER DREAMED OF BUILDING YOUR OWN BENCH but wondered where to start or were reluctant to do it on your own, there's help at any number of woodworking schools around the country. Courses range from intensive, five-day workshops to basic woodworking programs lasting several months or more, where bench-building is just one aspect of the class. Instructors will walk you through the process of making a classic workbench, including adding various vise configurations and other holding systems. Materials are usually included in the fee. The result is a workhorse that typically costs half as much as a commercial bench and one you can proudly call your own.

▲ BUILT WITH HELP. In as little as five days, you can build a dream bench at a woodworking school under an instructor's watchful eye and come home with a rock-solid beauty. Spence DePauw's maple workbench was constructed at American Sycamore Woodworkers' Retreat and features a sturdy trestle-style base, two vises, and double rows of dog holes.

A Chair for the Bench

WHILE MOST BENCHWORK DEMANDS THAT YOU STAND, it's nice to sit occasionally for certain tasks. Sitting can offer more precision, such as when laying out or cutting joints and when doing any type of detailed work. If you have a bad back, a good chair can relieve back strain. Or perhaps you simply want to sit at the bench and design or doodle a sketch or two. Unfortunately, standard chairs with seat heights of 16 in. to 18 in. are designed for tables and desks, not for the higher surface of a workbench. The key is to find a higher seat. One that adjusts to suit your particular bench height is ideal.

There are several adjustable stools and chairs that work well for the shop. One particularly convenient apparatus is the Best Hobby Chair, made from lightweight steel tubing with a fully adjustable wooden seat. Lowering or raising the seat is a snap, and the chair transports and stores easily, thanks to its folding-frame design. If a comfy perch is important to you, be sure to check it out.

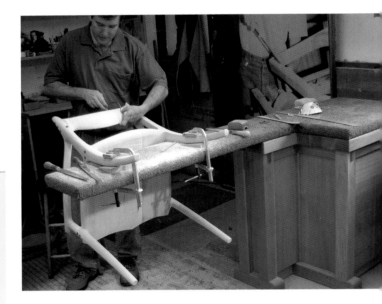

▲ OUT ON A LIMB. Holding odd-shaped work, such as chairs, is no problem with a top that extends past its base. Mike Johnson's chairmaking bench offers access on all sides for various clamping setups. Loading heavy gear in the bench's cabinet keeps the cantilevered worktop stable.

▲ CRANK IT UP. A height-adjustable bench offers more precision in your work and can relieve back strain. Curtis Erpelding's design lifts the top via four threaded rods implanted in the legs. A removable handwheel connected to a chain (hidden under the benchtop) lets you adjust the height without strain.

▲ SIT AT THE HEIGHT YOU LIKE. A seat that adjusts in height lets you tailor a work chair to the height of your bench. Seat height on the Best Hobby Chair ranges from 14 in. to 25 in. and then stows flat against the frame, taking up little space for storage.

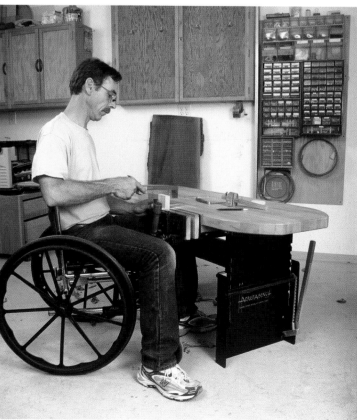

LIFT OR STEP TO HEIGHT. Rout, carve, and cut joints on a high surface, or handplane and assemble down low—even while sitting down—with the ADJUSTABENCH, which adjusts from 27 in. to about 44 in. Raise the bench by simply lifting the top; step on a foot pedal to lower its height. There's even a hand-operated height mechanism available for handicapped users.

▲ WEIGHT IT OUT. Metal lathes, and even wood lathes, will benefit from a heavy mass supporting the work to reduce vibration. Jim Moon's lathe bench is stout and sturdy, and drawers filled with gear ensure smooth operation above while the works spins.

◄ ▲ CHOP WHILE YOU SIT. Topping a standard chairmaker's shaving horse with a wood slab allows you to cut joints and perform other pounding tasks without moving to your main bench. Russ Filbeck's maple top connects in seconds and is drilled with holes that engage holdfasts for secure clamping.

▲ ▶ WORKING IN A BREEZE. A portable bench lets you take it to the job site or simply work outdoors when weather permits. The natural pole legs in the author's bench are tapered to fit tapered, through-mortises in the slab top, making a solid connection that knocks down in seconds for easy transport. Holes in the slab accommodate holdfasts, while an extra hole filled with beeswax provides ready lubricant for hand tools, screws, and other hardware.

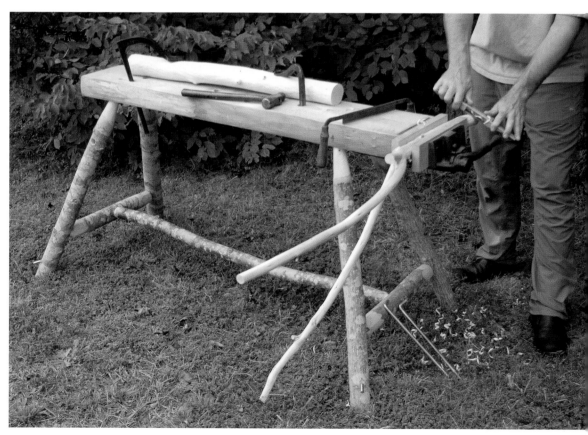

◄ A REALLY LONG BENCH. **Built-in cabinets topped with long counters let you organize tools and supplies, while affording plenty of bench space on which to work. Countertop material can be sturdy panels of MDF or plywood, edged with solid wood.**

► COUNTER MOVES. **Portable countertop cabinets allow you to arrange shop space as you see fit. The author's birch-plywood cabinet stores a ton of tools and is capped with a slab of hard maple for heavy use and long wear.**

◄ PREP COUNTER. Counters are handy workstations for general cleanup and sharpening tasks, or even food prep, when stocked with the necessary gear. Spence DePauw's base cabinet and countertop share space with a fridge and utility sink, making sharpening chores, finish cleanup, and the occasional snack more convenient.

FREESTANDING COUNTER

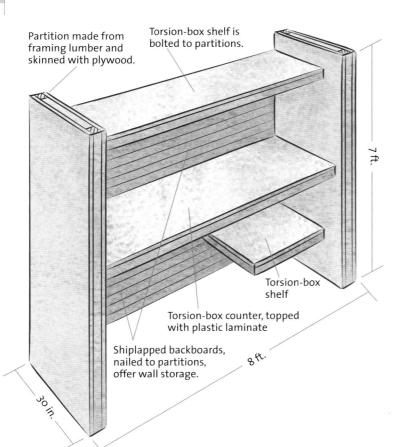

Partition made from framing lumber and skinned with plywood.

Torsion-box shelf is bolted to partitions.

7 ft.

Torsion-box shelf

Torsion-box counter, topped with plastic laminate

Shiplapped backboards, nailed to partitions, offer wall storage.

8 ft.

30 in.

▲ COUNTER IN SPACE. A freestanding partition with counter space built in lets you divide the shop where you want, while adding a work surface in the bargain. Instead of building permanent walls, Mark Bellonby constructed two partitions with horizontal wall boards, a shelf, and a countertop between them.

Installing a Countertop

BUILT-IN COUNTERS ARE EASIER TO INSTALL than you might think. Plywood is an excellent choice for counter material, and adding a solid-wood lipping at the front will cover the raw edge while adding stiffness. For a secure connection, make sure to screw the counter into wood studs in the wall, or use masonry fasteners if you're drilling into brick, stone, or other masonry material.

If you glue a cleat under the counter at the back, you'll simplify installation. Simply draw a level line along the wall using a level, line up the counter with the line, and screw through the cleat and into the wall to install. To support the weight at the counter's front edge, install wood or metal braces every 2 ft. or so.

▲ STRONG ENOUGH TO STAND ON. Screws driven into the counter through the utility cabinets on either end help hold it in place. But the most important support is underneath, from a pair of metal brackets and a full-length cleat screwed to the wall.

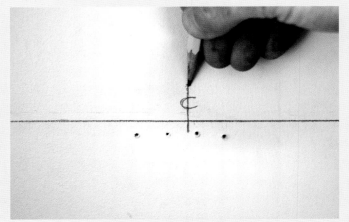

▲ LEVEL LAYOUT. The first steps to attaching a countertop are to mark a level line at the height of the counter and to find the studs in the wall. Use a nail or awl to poke through the wallboard until you strike solid wood, then mark each stud's centerline.

▲ PREDRILL THE CLEAT. A plywood cleat glued underneath the counter at the back will carry most of the rear weight, while metal braces support the front. Transfer the stud marks to the cleat, then use a countersink bit to drill through the cleat for screws.

▲ CAP IT WITH A SPLASH. You can add a plywood backsplash, which cleans up the joint line and protects the wall. Capping the splash itself with a strip of wood creates a mini shelf. Secure the splash to the studs in the wall with finish nails, and fill the holes with putty for a finished look.

Assembly Tables

OUNTERS AND WORKBENCHES OFTEN FALL SHORT when it comes time to assemble furniture and cabinets. Their relatively narrow widths and high work surfaces can make accurate assembly a chore, forcing you to prop up parts precariously or work on tiptoe to get a grip on clamps and other assembly procedures.

If you build a lot of case goods, a low bench is worth the time it takes to build, providing you with more control over the assembly process without straining your back. If you want to keep glue and other sticky stuff away from your main bench, a dedicated glue-up table might be in the cards.

When space is a premium, consider a knockdown design that you can store once you've assembled a project or a fold-up bench that supports your work and then folds out of the way, keeping shop clutter to a minimum.

▲ BUILD DOWN LOW. **A low setup table is a versatile companion to your main bench.** The top on Frank Klausz's 27-in.-high assembly table measures 40 in. by 60 in. and provides a handy surface for assembling casework, while organizing hardware and tools in drawers, bins, and cubbies.

▲ ▶ KEEPING CLEAN. **Controlling the mess is an important aspect of glue-up work.** John McDermott's glue-up table sports a hollow-core door faced with a sheet of vinyl-coated plywood to resist glue. The posts of the cart fit into holes drilled in stretchers under the top for a low-tech connection.

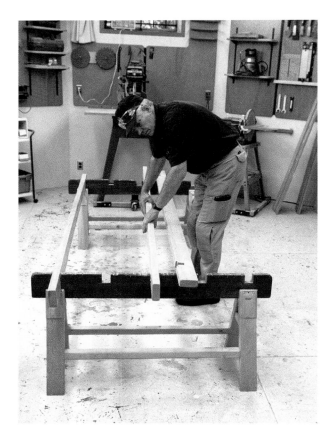

▲ ▶ PONIES ON THE GO. Sawhorses make an excellent temporary worktable when space is tight. Jan Carr's utility table sets up in seconds by fitting notched 2x4s into crossbeams on the horses. Half sheets of ¾-in. plywood provide a sturdy base surface, while a clean sheet of ¼-in. plywood on top protects the work.

▲ ▶ A BENCH THAT GROWS. Gain extra assembly room with a flip-up table, then stow it when floor space is needed. The hinged legs on Jan Derr's bench fold up under its hinged, drop-down top. Work surfaces are covered in plastic laminate to resist wear and glue.

Resources

Workbench Manufacturers

Carlsson Workbenches
Qvarnsövägen 25
570 83 Rosenfors, Sweden
049520662
www.winglink.com/mhb/english/

Find workbenches with wooden vise screws made in Sweden. This is the company that made the bench Ejler Hjorth-Westh uses.

Workbench World
9 Blaikie Street Unit 5
Myaree, Western Australia 6154
61 8 9330 5758
www.workbenchworld.com.au

This Australian bench maker builds a line of benches that runs the gamut from mechanics' benches to those for woodworkers. They build kits, benches to order in addition to their stock line.

Diefenbach Workbenches
33498 East US Highway 50
Pueblo, CO 81006
800-322-3624
www.workbenches.com

A full line of German made workbenches is found here. The company will make special benches to order, for example a left-handed bench with the vise locations reversed from the normal configuration.

Ulmia
Altheimer Str. 1
D-88515 Langenenslingen, Germany
49 (0) 7371/966920
www.ulmia.de

German benches, accessories, tools, and hardware are found here.

Laguna Tool
17101 Murphy Avenue
Irvine, CA 92614
949-474-1200
www.lagunatools.com

Laguna Tool carries a full range of workbenches and stationary power tools imported from Europe.

Tools and Portable Benches

Festool USA
Tooltechnic Systems, LLC
140 Los Carneros Way
Goleta, CA 93117
888-337-8600
www.festool-usa.com

Festool carries full line of very high quality power woodworking tools made in Europe including a fold-out portable bench They have sales outlets in nearly every state.

Lie-Nielsen Toolworks
P.O. Box 9
Warren, ME 04864-0009
800-327-2520
www.lienielsen.com

Lie-Nielsen sells very high quality hand tools, replacement parts like plane irons, and books on woodworking. Don't miss the section about the use and care of individual tools on their Web site.

Retailers

Woodcraft
P.O. Box 1686
Parkersburg, WV 26102-1686
800-225-1153
www.woodcraft.com

Woodcraft carries the full line of Sjöberg benches. They also carry the quick-release front vise hardware I used for the bench in Chapter 9 and good-quality screws for tail vises and shoulder vises. There are 74 stores nationwide.

Woodworkers Supply
5604 Alameda Place NE
Albuquerque, NM 87113
800-645-9292
www.woodworkerssupply.com

One of the largest woodworking product lines, Woodworkers Supply carries bench plans, vises (including a quick-action front vise mechanism), Jorgenson vises, and thousands of cabinet hardware items. There are stores in Albuquerque, NM; Casper, WY; and Graham, NC.

Garrett Wade
161 Avenue of the Americas
New York, NY 10013
800-221-2942
www.garrettwade.com

For decades, the New York-based Garrett Wade company has sold workbenches, accessories, tools and hardware. A leader in workbench development, Gary Chinn will be happy to special order any Ulmia bench you find on the Ulmia Web site.

Grizzly Industrial, Inc.
800-523-4777
www.grizzly.com

Grizzly carries premade butcher-block tops, metal bases, tools, machines, and hardware. They have a great Web site and catalog, showing the truly amazing range of machinery, tools, and equipment they carry. Showrooms in Springfield, MO; Muncy, PA; and Bellingham, WA. Don't miss the chance to see their gigantic showroom in Springfield, MO.

Hartville Tool
Hartville Hardware
940 West Maple Street
Hartville, OH 44632
800-345-2396
www.hartvilletool.com

Hartville Tool carries workbench plans, accessories, vises, and hardware. They have the Wilton quick-action front vise and the Jorgenson quick-action front vise in two sizes.

Highland Hardware
1045 North Highland Avenue NE
Atlanta, GA 30306
800-241-6748
www.highlandhardware.com

Highland Hardware carries the Hoffman and Hammer line of workbenches, Veritas vises and accessories, 2¼-in.-thick maple butcher block bench tops, tools, and hardware galore.

Lee Valley
Lee Valley Tools Ltd.
P.O. Box 1780
Ogdensburg, NY 13669-6780
OR:
P.O. Box 6295, Station J
Ottawa, ON K2A 1T4 Canada
800-871-8158
www.leevalley.com

Lee Valley carries the Veritas line of workbenches, the twin-screw end vise, the Tucker pattern-maker's vise, bench plans, cast-iron bases, bench accessories, hold-downs, and hardware. Their site offers lots of wood-working tips.

Rockler Woodworking and Hardware
4365 Willow Drive
Medina, MN 55340
800-279-4441
www.rockler.com

Rockler carries Sjöberg work-benches, lots of bench accessories tools, and hardware. They have stores nationwide and a great Web site and catalog. Rockler has the full line of T track hardware and accessories.